Innovation without Change?

Consumer Power in Psychiatric Services

David Brandon

M

MACMILLAN

First published 1991

Published by
MACMILLAN EDUCATION LTD
Houndmills, Basingstoke, Hampshire RG21 2XS
and London
Companies and representatives
throughout the world

Edited and typeset by Povey/Edmondson
Okehampton and Rochdale, England

Printed in Hong Kong

British Library Cataloguing in Publication Data
Brandon, David 1941–
Innovation without change?: consumer power in
psychiatric services.
1. Mentally ill persons. Care
I. Title
362.20425
ISBN 0–333–48823–7 (hardcover)
ISBN 0–333–48824–5 (paperback)

This book is dedicated to the memory of John Perceval, founder of the Alleged Lunatics Friends Society in 1845 and great grandfather of the English mental illness service reform movements

Contents

Acknowledgements

I owe many thanks to Malcolm Rae, psychiatric nurse and Prestonian *par excellence*; Lindsey Dyer, long-time friend and Director of North West MIND; Shula Ramon, Peter Campbell, Ingrid Barker, Jan Wallcraft, Peter Beresford, Suzy Croft, Edith Morgan and Wout Hardeman from Holland.

I owe much love to my wife Althea for all her support.

It is none of these people's fault that this book is not much much better.

DAVID BRANDON

1

Introduction

It seems that substantial changes are taking place in the mental illness services. 'Community care' has been a rallying cry for several decades. Large mental hospitals decrease in size and some close. Community psychiatric nursing develops as a profession. District General Hospital psychiatric units open in large numbers. Hostels and day centres open in many towns. The professional literature buzzes with terms like 'empowerment' and 'advocacy'. Long-neglected psychiatric patients have suddenly been magicked into service consumers, presumably active participants in service development. It seems that mental illness services are shaken by major changes at every level.

Does all that talk and writing amount to more than a hill of beans? Is it image or substance? Is it activity or action: hustle or bustle? Are the lunatics really taking over the asylums? Do service consumers experience any real differences at the sharp end? Do they feel any more involved in the services; have more influence in the kind of treatment they receive; get more information about what is happening; are their complaints taken more seriously? Or is it just the same old paternalism and imperialism with a fresh coat of paint? Perhaps the people, both staff and patients, are shaken but not stirred?

An American psychologist, Anthony M. Graziano, used the haunting phrase 'innovation without change'. He suggested that the

> conception of innovative ideas in mental health depends upon creative humanitarian and scientific forces, while their implementation depends, not on science and humanitarianism, but on a broad spectrum of professional and social politics! . . . these

1

two aspects, conceiving innovation through science and huma-
nitarianism on the other hand, are directly incompatible and
mutually inhibiting factors; our pursuit of political power has
almost totally replaced humanitarian and scientific ideals in the
mental health field. Innovations, by definition, introduce change;
political power structures resist change. Thus, while the cry for
innovation has been heard throughout the 1960s, we must clearly
recognise that it has been innovative 'talking' which has been
encouraged, while innovative action has been resisted. (Graziano,
1968)

This book examines the struggle which Graziano outlined
towards the end of the 1960s, and sees, in the context of user
influence in the mental illness field, whether it is still true of the late
1980s and likely to be valid for the 1990s. I write primarily from
the experience of the wounded healer, who has been both sides of
the large service divide – as a nursing assistant in mental hospitals,
hostel warden, Director of North West MIND and as a local
authority psychiatric social worker and now currently a psychotherapist – but most importantly as a psychiatric patient whose
father was also one. It is that latter experience which has been the
more memorable and influential and mainly drives this study.

I recall visiting him in the late 1950s. He was in the admission
unit of the Cherry Knowles mental hospital, Ryhope, near
Sunderland. The place smelled of stale urine, fresh floor polish
and the sickly sweet perfume of the tranquilliser Paraldehyde.
Pumped full of Paradelhyde, he was a walking dead man; all the
life drained from him, hard to recognise my Dad, so often feared,
detested and even sometimes loved.

Much seems to have changed since then. There can be little
argument about the substantial noise in the field of mental illness,
but is it a symphony or a cacophony? Often it is hard to hear
oneself speak. Everywhere, in nursing, psychiatry, psychology,
social work, there is the hustle and excitement of innovation.
New ideas, new treatments, new therapies, new service structures
abound. Services are moving, not without trauma, into 'community care'- whatever that immensely elastic term is taken to mean.
But does that mean radical challenges to traditional imperialistic
professional practices and values? Does it mean changing centuries
of history consisting mainly of degradation and inhumanity?

Susan Clayton warns us that all is not as it appears. Current slogans and banners are used for complex purposes. 'Attempts to gain consumer views in the health service reflect a variety of aims which are not necessarily in the consumer's interests' (Clayton, 1988). She suggests that these aims may include an enhancement of decision-making by authorities or the gaining of information to control more effectively practitioners, managers, and in their turn, consumers. Another aim may be to help people feel better because they have had the chance to say something, rather than really influence services – ventilation rather than actual power and responsibility.

This book resembles a plumber's handbook. It analyses some blocks and suggests ways of freeing the pipes. It takes no great philosophical flights about the nature, substance and causes of mental illness. This agnostic author has few gifts and none are in that direction. The book is concerned about the present and what can be done, largely in a reformist way, to improve the experience of people within the services. I include most staff in that description. The mental illness services are a major disappointment to many who come to work within them.

This study is mainly concerned with the longer-stay patients rather than those with briefer experiences of the services. That should not imply any denial of their obvious distress. More and more people are unnecessarily defined as 'mentally ill'.

People who look strange or behave oddly threaten any society until their uncommon traits have been formally named and their uncommon behaviour has been slotted into a recognised role. By being assigned a name and a role, eerie and upsetting deviants are turned into well-defined and established categories. In industrial societies the abnormal is entitled to special consumption. Medical labelling has increased the number of people with exceptional consumer status to the point where people who are free of therapy-oriented labels have become the exception. (Illich, 1974)

In the main, I have avoided using the fashionable terms 'empowerment' and 'consumers', partly because like the other ersatz term 'befriending' they sell us short. Do terms like empowerment and befriending amount to full friendship and full power? If they do, then why not just call it friendship and taking power and control?

First, in Chapter 2, this book traces the sketchy history of lunatics/patients within the mental illness service – from the trial as a heretic of Margery Kempe in the early fifteenth century to *One Flew Over the Cuckoo's Nest*, the best-selling novel and popular film. It looks at what they wrote and said, usually overpowered by the extensive palaeontology of the various professionals – largely doctors and reformers – their books and case studies. It focuses mainly on the users' experiences of the services, rather than on the experience of madness/mental illness, more fully documented particularly by professionals. Mostly, users had a hard time at the hands of the lunacy/mental illness services. Often the nature of the treatment was rather more damaging than the nature of the illness. It seemed closer to cruel punishment than genuine compassion. They felt confused and violated. Other people were afraid of them. Those uncomfortable voices and the screams and sobbings of patients have, for the most part, gone unheard by professionals and policy-makers, who felt they knew best.

Chapter 3, 'Wind and Tides', looks at the immense forces which surround the mental illness services and impel some sort of major transformation. Huge currents like 'consumerism', the principle of normalisation, anti-psychiatry and de-professionalism have direct and far-reaching implications for mental illness services. Psychiatric services operate within an overall context of a social and economic structure, particularly of changes in the demands for labour.

The 'Mismatch' chapter (Chapter 4) looks at the modern experiences of mental hospital patients and the resistances to change from professionals. It examines how nurses, social workers and others are trained and socialised; their fears and anxieties; what they believe; the jargon barriers; and the increasing social distance between patients and relatives and those who run the services. It studies the links between genuine caring, sensitivity and self-interest and control. It examines the conflicts between professionals and the increasing pressures from a more 'consumerist' society. Mental illness is the most intensely resistant of the client group empires against radical change. Why should that be?

Chapters 5 to 8 have the common themes of openness and resistance. They examine the progress and resistances to more open and democratic systems – some basic problems of information, consultation, advocacy and democratisation. What principles should govern telling patients and their relatives about their situations? Are there good and clear ethical grounds on which to withhold information? Who should make those decisions and how?

By what methods do we provide effective and independent advocacy for people often unable to be effective self-advocates at times of maximum stress? We look at the vested interests of professionals which prevent them being effective advocates. How do we handle more wisely this heady mixture of care and control? How do we help users, particularly those with chronic disabilities and who have become institutionalised, to become more assertive – through self-advocacy, for example? How can we help staff to be less afraid of criticism?

How can we make our services more democratic and accountable? We look at the democratisation of services and the problems for staff. Among several promising new systems, we examine the Canadian system of service brokerage, which offers the possibility of people getting cash and independent professional assistance from service brokers, to take responsibility for running their own services. Each chapter suggests small breakthroughs – good news from various areas like Chesterfield and Nottingham, and further afield in the USA, Italy and Holland.

The conclusion tries to summarise both the hope and the despair. It looks at the possible implications of the Government White Paper *Caring for People*. It looks at the role of professionalism and imagines new forms of training and practice. Amid the fields of deadly nightshade, there are some primroses. There is not just much innovation but a little real change.

The most important and relevant symptoms of mental illness are frequently poverty and powerlessness. People lack the means to live reasonably securely; often losing their regular paid work. They face stigma based on fear from friends and neighbours. We must find a way to give people with disabilities, especially those with mental illness, a more reasonable share of this wealthy society's riches than in the last several centuries. We must find ways of ensuring that those people who feel 'out of control', powerless over their thoughts and feelings, are not made to feel even more vulnerable by the very structures which are ostensibly designed to help them.

Consider these sensitive words:

A successful, open and confident society tolerates wide varia-
tions in thought and behaviour. A society under stress becomes
less tolerant. The forces of law become more vigilant or
oppressive, depending on the view taken. But the process is
not limited to the forces of law. Others involved in the
maintenance of the prevailing social values are pressed into
aid. Mental illness experts are among them. Political differences
can become deviance, a code word on occasions for illness.
Social protest can become irrational and dangerous behaviour.
The black man who makes a speech calling for the destruction of
the 'white devils' will be 'remanded' for a psychiatric report.
Sexual predilections can become sick depravities. We begin to
see madness as a metaphor for those things we disapprove of in
our society. Suddenly, the metaphor takes on a life of its own.
That which was metaphor now becomes illness. (Kennedy, 1981)

References

Susan Clayton, 'Patient Participation: An Underdeveloped Concept',
    Journal of the Royal Society of Health (1988).
Anthony M. Graziano, 'Clinical Innovation and Mental Health Power
    Structure: A Social Case History', Paper presented at the meeting of the
    Eastern (USA) Psychological Association, Washington D.C. (April
    1968) p. 2.
Ivan Illich, *Medical Nemesis – The Expropriation of Health* (Calder &
    Boyars, 1975).
Ian Kennedy, *The Unmasking of Medicine* (Allen & Unwin, 1981) p. 108.

2

Lunatics and Asylums

The history of the mental illness services is dominated by reformers and paid professionals – the keepers, nurses, psychiatrists, etc. Rarely is the voice of the 'lunatic' heard except through the traditional case studies, where little sense of a whole person is ever revealed – only a ragbag of unusual symptoms to illustrate some treasured thesis of the writer. We hear the voice of the victors, not that of the victims, and rarely appreciate the intimate and subtle relationships between them. There is some deep truth in that caustic comment of Florence Nightingale about Shaftesbury, the nineteenth-century social reformer: 'Lord Shaftesbury would have been in an asylum had he not devoted himself to reforming them' (Skultans, 1979, p. 98). Professionals and patients, keepers and lunatics, develop a strange sort of dependency on one another.

Without the earthiness and realism provided by generations of patients and their relatives, the historical literature takes flights and fancies motivated more by career ambitions and the medicalisation of insanity than by people's suffering and the changing cultures in which they lived. For the most part, studies of insanity over the centuries have developed powerful myths, established a huge industry which adds to the stigmatising of a section of the population.

Madness has become increasingly strange and remote from the ordinary lives of people. Michel Foucault comments:

In the Renaissance, madness was everywhere and mingled with every experience by its images and its dangers. During the classical period, madness was shown, but on the other side of the bars, if present, it was at a distance, under the eyes of a

7

reason that no longer felt any relation to it and that would not compromise itself by too close a resemblance. (Foucault, 1971, p. 70)

throughout Europe, confinement had the same meaning, at least if we consider its origins. It constituted one of the answers the seventeenth century gave to the economic crisis that affected the entire Western world: reduction of wages, unemployment, scarcity of coin. (Foucault, 1971, p. 49)

The mad were increasingly marginalised both economically and socially.

People were not incarcerated because of their madness. In 1844 more than 80 per cent of those diagnosed as insane were classified as paupers (Scull, 1982, p. 226). Between 1844 and 1860, the number of pauper lunatics rose by 96.4 per cent compared with 24.4 per cent amongst private lunatics.

It was difficult for either physicians or reformers to see the immense socio-economic forces involved in the growth of the lunacy trade. Observers as perceptive as Matthew Allen, superintendent of the High Beech madhouse in Essex, which the poet John Clare entered in 1837, were rare (Blunden, 1931). 'I had then not the slightest hesitation in saying that if a small pension could be obtained for him, he would have recovered instantly and probably have remained well for life.' Instead John Clare spent the rest of this life in asylums. Whilst Allen encouraged Clare's poetic genius, one Peterborough doctor who had treated him decided that his madness was caused by 'years addicted to Poetic prosings'. It was common to stress the culpability of individuals for their mental condition and ignore the structural forces.

Increasingly, poor people were dumped in institutions. The boundaries of insanity were gradually and considerably extended over the centuries. Segregation of mad people meant that that tolerance of ordinary local people to strange behaviour was gradually reduced. Madness became a phenomenon which only 'special' experts in preferably isolated buildings could handle.

Patients were no longer real human beings. Increasing incarceration and confinement made them seem more inhuman and grotesque. Some forms of human distress and anger became symptoms of complex psychiatric syndromes to be managed and cured by complicated and unpleasant medicines, isolation and sometimes cruel treatment. Thousands of paying visitors to Bethlem mocked and jeered the lunatics. Tom o' Bedlam was a powerful image in Shakespeare's *King Lear*. Edward Wakefield visiting Bethlem in 1815 saw the lunatic William Norris. 'He was held by a chain around his neck with the other end attached to the wall. He could not either stand or lie flat and had been like that for nine years.' Unsurprisingly, he was totally emaciated and had chronic TB (Skultans, 1979, p. 110).

The professionals effectively rendered their patients mute. Because of prevailing beliefs that madness was close to evil, chaos, sin and so-called sexual perversion, they devalued and largely ignored their views. For many professionals, even ordinary conversation was irrelevant. In 1758, Dr Battie of the St Luke's Asylum, south London, spoke sternly of the 'impertinent curiosity of those who think it positive to converse with Madmen and to play on their other passions'.

Theories about the aetiology of madness varied exotically. Among the first accounts by a 'patient' was that of Margery Kempe, largely written down probably by her son, in 1436. She was the daughter of the Mayor of Lynn in Norfolk. She was born in 1373 and married young. Soon after the birth of her first child in 1393 she 'went out of her mind for about eight months, during which time she saw flame-tongued devils'. In 1413 she went on a pilgrimage to Rome and the Holy Land, dressed in white according to 'a divine injunction'. Upon arriving in Jerusalem she began 'crying and roaring though she should have died for it'. Some people assumed she was ill. Some thought she had the 'falling evil' – presumably epilepsy. Others felt she was possessed by the Devil or was a heretic because her behaviour was linked with religious themes. In 1417 she was brought to trial for heresy in the Church of All Hallows at Leicester, but on examination she appeared orthodox and was acquitted, saved from death by fire (Peterson, 1982, pp. 6–18).

Timothy Bright in his *Treatise of Melancholy* (1586) linked melancholy with sinfulness (Jones, 1972, p. 41). 'Although no man is by nature freed from this affliction in so much as all men are sinners and being culpable of the breech of God's laws, incurre the punishment of condemnations yet is the melancholicke person more than any subject thereunto . . .' The Danish theologian, with a long history of depression, Soren Kierkegaard, living in the first half of the nineteenth century, was more equivocal about the connection. 'The worst affliction of all is, and continues to be, that one does not know whether one's suffering is an illness of the mind or a sin' (Jaspars, 1923, p. 425).

In 1621, Robert Burton, a lifelong batchelor, saw women as driving men to insanity. 'That other madness is a woman . . . Pleasant at first she is, that fair plant in the eye, but poison to the taste, the rest as bitter as woodworm in the end, and sharp as a two-edged sword. Her house is the way to Hell, and goes down to the chamber of death' (Burton, 1621).

None of the few lunatics whose writings survive were poor. They were either aristocrats or wounded healers – doctors or clergymen who had had a breakdown. Their history contrasts with the vast bulk of material provided by professionals and reformers. Take the situation of John Clare, the peasant-poet, who on leaving High Beech madhouse spent his last twenty-seven years in Northampton County Asylum. Its superintendent Prichard wrote in 1845: 'He enjoys perfect liberty here and passes all his time out of doors in the field or town, returning home only to his meals and bed.' An idyllic picture. But in the same year Clare writes to his wife Patty: 'This is an English Bastille . . . where harmless people are trapped and tortured till they die – English bondage more severe than the slavery of Egypt and Africa.' (Tibble, 1932, p. 421). Clearly one of these two is deluded!

The history of English mental illness services until the early eighteenth century is largely the history of the Bethlem Hospital in London. Bethlem, or Bedlam, derived its name from the priory of the Order of St Mary of Bethlehem founded in London in 1247, appropriated by the Crown in 1375 and two years later used as an institution for those with acute forms of mental illness. Provision was on a modest scale (Scull, 1982, p. 19). In 1403–4, the inmates consisted of six insane patients and three sane patients, and this number grew slowly. In 1632, it held twenty-seven patients, and by 1642, forty-four.

In 1733, Hogarth painted conditions in the Bethlem incurable ward in *The Rake's Progress*. The unfortunate Rake lies on the stone floor, practically naked with his head shaven, whilst a keeper manacles his feet and an apothecary examines his head. Gilman shows how paintings and, later, photography powerfully influenced the perceptions of madness. His assiduously researched work shows a mass of images, from Alberti's *Madwoman Confronting Attila* (1690) to Wiertz's *Hunger, Madness, Crime* (1864) and beyond (Gilman, 1982). The portrayals point to extremes: too much movement, gesture and screaming, towards too little – withdrawal and silence; immensely powerful stereotypes.

Foucault sees a sudden change in the world of madness in the middle of the seventeenth century. Before this change, madness was allowed free range with exceptional cases treated in madhouses. Afterwards, 'the world of madness was to become the world of exclusion' (Foucault, 1976, pp. 67–8). The workhouses of Britain housed more and more mad people in overcrowded and worsening conditions.

Those who posed a particularly acute threat to the social order, or lacked friends or family on whom they could call for support, were likely to find themselves, along with the 'sick, aged, bed-ridden, diseased, wayfaring men, diseased soldiers, and honest folk fallen into poverty', cared and provided for within the walls of one of the many small medieval 'hospitals'. Custody for others who proved too violent and unmanageable to be maintained in the community was provided in the local gaol.

One origin of madhouses for pauper lunatics was the development in some parishes from the mid seventeenth century of boarding them out, 'at the expense of the parish, in dwelling houses, which gradually acquired the description of private "mad" houses'. Among the more affluent classes, patients were placed by their families to be cared for on an individual basis, frequently 'in the custody of medical men or clergymen' (Parry-Jones, 1972). This has a strangely contemporary ring.

The Revd George Trosse (1631–1713) tells of his involuntary admission to a private madhouse. 'I heard the voice of God asking me to be more and more humble. I took off my stockings and bowed low, sprinkling earth and dust on my head and was filled with grievous Horrour and Anguish, with great Anxiety and sinking Despair.' After an immense struggle, his friends had him admitted to a private madhouse near Glastonbury. He felt he was going to Hell:

> Hereupon, my Friends determin'd to remove me to his House, but I was resolv'd not to move out of my Bed; for I was

perswaded that if I removed out of it, I should fall into Hell, and
be plung'd into the Depth of Misery . . . Therefore I stoutly
resisted them, with all my Might and utmost Efforts, and
struggled with all Violence, that they might not pluck me out
of my Bed and cloath me. (Hunter and MacAlpine, 1963)

He was there for some weeks or months, 'full of Horror, Delusions
and Blasphemy'. The keeper sometimes put bolts on his hands and
fetters on his feet. Eventually he became quieter, more composed
and regained his liberty. Hare suggests that Trosse was not
schizophrenic but had an alcoholic psychosis with an affective
disorder (Hare, 1988).

Timothy Rogers (1658–1728), a Nonconformist Minister and
contemporary of Trosse, wrote a pamphlet called 'Advices to
Friends of Melancholy People' (Hunter and MacAlpine, 1963,
pp. 248–51). He knew of no effective medicine for the condition.
He had had a breakdown in his early twenties – 'a deep and settled
melancholly' which lasted two years. 'Melancholly seizes on the
Brain and Spirits, and incapacitates them for Thought and Action;
it confounds and disturbs all their thoughts, and unavoidably fills
them with anguish and vexation.'

Rogers values 'wounded healers'. He advises people to use
'Doctors who have suffered from Melancholly':

It is impossible to understand the nature of it in any other way
than by Experience . . . Look at those with Melancholly with
pity and compassion . . . Do not attribute the effects of the
Disease to the Devil . . . Tell them of others who have been in
such Anguish, and under such a terrible Distemper, and yet have
been delivered. (Hunter and MacAlpine, 1963)

These are vital themes finding little echo in the professional
literature.

Goodwin Wharton was an MP from 1690 until his death in 1704.
He did not see himself as mad and never received treatment as far
as we know. He wrote a monumental autobiography from 1686
onwards which is a testament of 'a mind enmeshed in the thickets
of delusion', dedicated to his phantom son, Peregrine. The story is

full of contact with spirits and fairies intermingled with a mass of sexual experiences (Porter, 1990).

Cruden's pamphlets begin the documentation of protest by lunatics themselves, although there is registered a lost pamphlet from 1620 entitled 'The Petition of the Poor Distracted People in the House of Bedlam' (Peterson, 1982, p. 47). Alexander Cruden, author of a major reference book on the Bible, wrote of his treatment and escape from Bethlem in 1739. He was locked in a cell, chained by one leg to a bedstead with handcuffs on his wrists. When he protested, the keepers put him in a 'strait-wastecoat' with hands tied behind his back and he was given 'purging physick'. He eventually escaped over a wall (Peterson, 1982, p. 358).

Urbane Metcalf was witness to considerable cruelty and theft by staff. He was a patient in Bedlam between 1804 and 1806, and then again in 1817, when he thought himself the son of Matilda, sister to the King of Denmark, an heir to the throne.

> I myself have not cause to complain as I was generally treated with great civility, but I am, from a sense of humanity, pleading the cause of the unfortunate . . . It would extend far beyond the limits of this little work to pourtray the villainies practised by the Jacks in office, bribery is common to them all; cruelty is common to them all; villainy is common to them all; in short every thing is common but virtue, which is so uncommon they take care to lock it up as a rarity. (Peterson, 1982)

Just after the passing of the 1774 Madhouses Act, a Stamford tradesman printed his pamphlet 'The Case, Petition and Address of Samuel Bruckshaw' followed by his 'One More Proof of the Iniquitous Abuse of Private Madhouses' published in the same year. He wrote about being locked up, though perfectly sane, as a consequence of a villainous conspiracy hatched by his commercial rivals. He writes of Wilson, his keeper in the madhouse:

> When Wilson shewed me to bed, he carried me up into a dark and dirty garret, there stripped me, and carried my cloathes out of the room, which I saw no more, for upwards of a month, but lay chained to this bad bed, all that time . . . In the daytime the window is darkened, and common necessities denied; they gave

me bad victuals, short allowance, with sour beer, oftener water, and sometimes not that; no attendance, but what was as contradictory and provoking as they could invent, and frequently the most barbarous stripes. (Peterson, 1982, pp. 57–64)

Similar complaints came from William Belcher in 1796 (Peterson, 1982). However, William Cowper, the poet, was more fortunate with his treatment for melancholia in a private madhouse in St Albans (1763–5): 'It was agreed among them [friends] that I should be carried to St Alban's where Dr Cotton kept a house for the reception of such patients, and with whom I was known to have a slight acquaintance. Not only his skill, as a physician, recommended him to their choice, but his well-known humanity, and sweetness of temper.' He says mysteriously, 'It will be proper to draw a veil over the secrets of my prison house; let it suffice to say, that the low state of body and mind, to which I was reduced, was perfectly well calculated to humble the natural vainglory and pride of my heart' (Peterson, 1982, pp. 64–73).

By the end of the eighteenth century, state intervention was increasing:

There was a growing market or trade in lunacy; and those operating in this developing market were at work in a social context in which claims to possess expertise and special competence were on general grounds likely to find a receptive audience. It is thus not surprising that the development and consolidation of institutional means of coping with madness parallels that of a professionalized group of managers of the mad. (Parry-Jones, 1972)

These professionals were the new moral managers reacting to the terrible conditions portrayed by Hogarth and many others. They accepted the madman as human but lacking in both self-restraint and discipline. For them he was essentially a moral problem. The most famous, the Quaker William Tuke, was appalled by a visit to a fellow Quaker in the York Asylum in 1792. The Select Committee of 1815 reporting on this asylum found that one damp cell housed thirteen incontinent patients in an area 12 feet by 7 feet 10 inches. The same Committee, commenting generally about private madhouses, noted 'Fetters and chains, mopping at the morning toilet, irregular meals, want of exercise, the influction of abusive words, contemptuous names, blows with the fist, or with straps, or with keys, formed an almost daily part of the lives of many unprotected beings' (Skultans, 1979).

William Tuke set up The Retreat in York in 1797. Tuke had two notions about the treatment of insanity: as much physical comfort as possible, in a setting of quietness and stillness (Glover, 1984, pp. 48–9). Tuke and the Frenchman Pinel were influential in persuading professionals that treatment lay in the development of control from within the mind of the madman rather than through external locks and handcuffs. Tuke's grandson Samuel wrote in 1813:

Insane persons generally possess a degree of control over their wayward propensities. Their intellectual, active and moral powers, are usually rather perverted and obliterated; and it happens, not infrequently, that one faculty only is affected. The disorder is sometimes still more partial, and can only be detected by erroneous views on one particular subject. On all others the mind appears to retain its wanted correctness. (Tuke, 1813)

A contemporary, John Conolly, Superintendent of the Hanwell Asylum, was sardonic about the moral asylums:

What would be the consequence, if we were to take a sane person, who had been accustomed to enjoy society, and . . . were to lock him up in a small house with a keeper for his only associate, and no place for exercise but a miserable garden? We should certainly not look for any improvement in his moral and intellectual condition. Can we reasonably expect that a treatment which would be injurious to a sane mind, should tend to restore a diseased one? (Conolly, 1830, pp. 4–5)

He criticised the new asylum managers:

they may point to the spaciousness of their grounds, to the variety of occupations and amusements prepared for their patients; to the excellence of their food and the convenience of their lodging; and urge that as little restraint is employed as is compatible with their safety: but the fault of the association of lunatics with each other, and the infrequency of any communication between the patient and persons of sound mind mars the whole design. (ibid, pp. 20–2)

Even to preserve the principles of moral management at a time when asylums were expanding considerably in numbers was extremely difficult. They became lunatic pauper warehouses. In 1827 there were nine asylums with an average size of 116 beds. The 1845 Lunatic Asylums Act set up a National Committee of Lunacy to visit every kind of asylum at frequent intervals. It was made compulsory to provide county asylums. The numbers of asylums increased to 66 by 1890 with an average size of 802 beds (Jones, 1955, p. 116).

John Arlidge noted the dangers:

In a colossal refuge for the insane, a patient may be said to lose his individuality and to become a member of a machine so put together, as to move with precise regularity, and invariable routine; a triumph of skill adapted to show how such unpromising materials as crazy men and women may be drilled into order and guided by rule, but not an apparatus calculated to restore their pristine self-governing existence. In all cases admitting of recovery, or of material amelioration, a gigantic asylum is a gigantic evil and figuratively speaking a manufactory of chronic insanity. (Arlidge, 1859)

One huge problem lay in recruiting quality staff. L. D. Smith comments about the early nineteenth century that keepers were of low status and poorly paid, with usually no relevant experience or training and frequently scapegoated for the poor quality of the asylums. He quotes Edwin Rickman, one-time patient in Duddeston Hall, an asylum near Birmingham:

Nothing is more calculated to disgust and increase the excitement of a convalescent and sensitive mind, than to be subject to the low, and necessarily ignorant talk of even the most civil, and for their situation in life, the best informed of the class chosen to perform the important duties of attendance and companionship. (L. D. Smith, 1988, p. 309)

The keepers received widely conflicting guidelines. Samuel Bakewell wrote: 'It is . . . necessary that the keeper should always be able control them, and to assert his bodily as well as mental superiority. Nothing is more important as that his authority ever then be complete and acknowledged' (Bakewell, 1833). Instilling fear into lunatics contrasted with John Conolly's rather more humane advice:

To a great extent the companions of patients helping to amuse and cheer them, to soothe and direct them; omitting no observations of their appearance, manners and language, reporting their wants and wishes to the physician, and not overlooking indications of amendment and all this they are required to do with cheerfulness and with a perfect control of temper. (Conolly, 1856, pp. 102–3)

By the mid nineteenth century the Lancaster Asylum had become one of the most famous moral treatment centres under the regime of Drs Gaskell and De Vitre. Walton comments soberly about Lancaster: 'It is clear that even the most carefully nurtured and firmly established of "moral treatment" regimes were vulnerable, in the long run, to the combined pressures of increased scale, cheese-paring economies, overworked medical superintendents, aging patient populations, undersupervised nursing staff.' But he adds that asylums may have been 'a sad departure from the ideals expressed by apostles of moral treatment and non-restraint; but at least they represented a much less uncomfortable alternative to the workhouses in which so many of the congenitally inept, socially incompetent, and derelicts were still being confined in 1870' (Walton, 1981, pp. 191–2).

From the Napoleonic Wars period (1810) comes Haslam's marvellous account of James Tilly Mathews, a patient in London's Bethlem Hospital from 1797. This is the first comprehensive study of a lunatic published by a professional. Mathews protested his sanity, and his family, friends and parish authorities petitioned for his release. Haslam's study was an attempt at rebuttal.

'Although his insanity was then most evident, yet his relatives did not possess the faculty of perceiving his disorder' – a lack of insight. Eventually Haslam was dismissed by the Bedlam governors in 1816, due to the scandalous condition of the asylum. Part of the evidence contributing to his dismissal lay in written complaints from Mathews and his relatives (Haslam, 1988, p. xiii).

John Perceval's personal observations of madness are crucial. His father was the Prime Minister assassinated by a madman in the House of Commons in 1812. He became 'deranged' in 1831, and his mother and brother arranged admission to an institution run by Dr Fox in Brislington, Gloucestershire. He was then transferred in May 1832 to a private madhouse in Sussex where he remained until early in 1834. He married a year later and went to Paris where he wrote about his experiences, publishing two volumes in 1838 and 1840 of *A Narrative of the Treatment Experienced by a Gentleman, During a State of Mental Derangement* (see Peterson, 1982, pp. 92–4).

He describes in careful detail the physical abuse that took place in Dr Fox's madhouse: beatings, excessive restraints, forced cold baths, and forced medical treatment.

Perceval summarises beautifully the extensive differences between his needs and what was provided:

> I needed quiet, I needed tranquillity, I needed security. I needed at times even seclusion. I could not obtain them . . . My will, my wishes, my repugnancies, my habits, my delicacy, my inclinations, my necessities were never once consulted . . . Then I hated, I despised, I was enraged, I became hardened, I was brutalised . . . I will be bound to say that the greatest part of the violence that occurs in lunatic asylums is to be attributed to the conduct of those who are dealing with the disease, not the disease itself . . . Because I did not respect myself, they disrespected me, whereas they should have brought me to my senses by greater reserve and respect. (Bateson, 1961)

John Perceval was the first English 'lunatic reformer'. His *Narrative* is a serious work of protest. Early in the first volume, Perceval asks readers, 'In the name of humanity, then, in the name of modesty, in the name of wisdom, I intreat you to place yourselves in the position of those whose sufferings I describe.' In 1838, he worked for the release of Richard Paternoster, patient in a Kensington madhouse and later author of the protest work *The Madhouse System* (1841). In 1839 he tried, unsuccessfully, to introduce reforming legislation in Parliament. In 1841 he became interested in the case of Dr Pearce, a patient in the criminal section of Bethlehem, and ten years later published Dr Pearce's *Poems – By a Prisoner in Bethlehem* to raise funds to make his life more comfortable. In 1844 and 1855 Perceval wrote and published two more short accounts of the unjust treatment of patients.

In 1845, he and a group of acquaintances founded the Alleged Lunatic's Friend Society. He became honorary secretary in the following year. In 1859 and 1860, he and other members of the society appeared before an investigative parliamentary committee, where he described himself as 'the attorney-general of all Her Majesty's madmen' (Peterson, 1982, footnote p. 93). If anyone should receive acknowledgement as the father of the mental illness reform movement, it is Perceval.

The Victorian asylums had largely failed to live up to early promises. Concern about their wretched conditions mirrored that in the previous century. Frequently, when it was acknowledged that asylums were run badly, it was explained in terms of the 'unpromising material' admitted rather than through service deficiencies. It was rarely understood that the institutionalisation of pauper lunatics in the huge warehouses had much to do with the serious problems of an increasingly urbanised and industrialised society. Large-scale confinement of lunatics 'marked a decisive event: the moment when madness was perceived on the social horizon of poverty, of incapacity to work, of inability to integrate within the group; the moment when madness began to rank among the problems of the city' (Foucault, 1971, p. 64).

Henry Maudsley, the most influential psychiatrist of his generation, applied the scientific methods borrowed from Darwin to the problems of insanity. The psychiatric Darwinists insisted on physical causes which linked with the laws of fitness and selection. Madness was a symptom of the impotent and the unfit – the subhumans. Maudsley described the important link between masturbation in early life and some forms of insanity: 'We have degenerate beings produced who as regards moral character are very much what eunuchs are represented to be – cunning, deceitful, liars, selfish, in fact, morally insane; while their physical and intellectual vigour is further damaged by *the exhausting vice*' (Maudsley, 1868).

The major metaphor of the Darwinists was that of the 'borderland' – shadowy territory between sanity and insanity. This territory was to be annexed as their professional domain. Mercier wrote, 'Insanity is a dissolution; it is a retrogression; it is a traversing of the path of development in a reverse direction. It is a peeling off of those superimposed layers of development which have been laboriously deposited by the process of evolution' (Mercier, 1910; in Skultans, 1910). Many so-called corrective treatments were close to torture.

Take, for example, the case of Marcia Hamilcar, in December 1907, a 57-year-old English schoolteacher who became severely depressed and was admitted to a private asylum. She was held prisoner for five weeks. They took away her clothes, cut off her hair, strapped her to the bed, and kept her bound in a kind of straitjacket. She had drugs forced on her and was fed only a pint of milk a day. After five weeks she had lost 25 pounds and was covered with bruises from beatings that the director of the 'nursing home' said were 'self-inflicted'. By then she probably did look mad – very thin, frightened, head shaved, and occasionally delirious, perhaps mainly from the large doses of drugs (Peterson, 1982). Treatment or punishment?

This treatment was based on the contemptuous attitudes displayed towards the mad. Contempt replaced the humanistic attitudes of the Victorians. The insane were now an inferior breed, segregated because of the fear of social degeneration, and linked with sin, immorality of all kinds and lack of self-control.

The First World War and 'shell-shock' challenged the moral links between insanity and fecklessness. Shell-shock was an emotional disturbance caused by the war itself and the chronic conditions of tension and fear in which escape was dishonourable. Dr Thomas Salmon wrote, 'The real source of wonder was not that neurosis should play such an important part in military life, but that so many men should find a satisfactory adjustment without its intervention' (Salmon, 1917). The pressures of the immensely hostile environment were obviously dominant.

The poet Wilfred Owen was admitted to a mental hospital through shell-shock. He wrote, in 'Mental Cases':

> These are men whose minds the Dead have ravished.
> Memory fingers in their hair of murders,
> Multitudinous murders they once witnessed.
> Wading sloughs of flesh these helpless wander,
> Treading blood from lungs that had loved laughter.
> Always they must see these things and hear them,
> Batter of guns and shatter of flying muscles,
> Carnage incomparable, and human squander
> Rucked too thick for these men's extrication.

Psycho-analysis became very influential. Dr W. H. R. Rivers wrote:

> It is a wonderful turn of fate that just as Freud's theory of the unconscious and the method of psycho-analysis founded upon it should be so hotly discussed, there should have occurred events which have produced on an enormous scale just those conditions of paralysis and contracture, phobias and obsession, which the theory was especially designed to explain. (Rivers, 1917)

Hardly a turn of fate!

In Henderson and Gillespie's classic *A Textbook of Psychiatry* first published in 1927, mental illness is defined as 'the cumulative result of unhealthy reactions of the individual's mind to its environment'. Health is intrinsically masculine – 'the healthy attitude to life's difficulties and problems is a direct, aggressive, matter-of-fact one, designed to overcome the difficulty once and for all' (Ramon, 1985, p. 69).

The fundamental importance of health was crucial to understanding mental illness. Intervention models meant: reducing life to the simplest level; early hospitalisation; bed rest; attention to physical condition; sleep and bath as relaxation and tonics; 'perhaps the most important thing of all . . . is to give the patient some better understanding of the factors responsible for the illness' (Ramon, 1985, p. 74).

Between the wars, few voices of psychiatric patients were heard publicly. One exception was Mr J. Jones MP, who saw the links with poverty. 'I might have been certified years ago but still think that I was as sane as anyone who has spoken tonight.' After this confession he was often treated as an oddity (Ramon, 1985, p. 74).

Dr D. Johnson, an MP in the 1950s, similarly confessed to having been an ex-mental patient and became a major campaigner for patients' civil rights. He was termed 'sensational' and 'irresponsible' by other MPs (Ramon, 1985, p. 229).

Case descriptions of mental patients were used in Parliament in the 1920s largely to make various political points. The descriptions stressed that patients had to be protected; they were helpless and weak; they needed practical help and sensitivity (Ramon, 1985, p. 115). Laing wrote of his fifty-year stay in Scottish mental hospitals, frequently starved and battered by staff. He was nine years old on admission in 1939. 'My dormitory was one of the smaller ones with sixteen beds. They were just bare dormitories with highly polished floors. There were no lockers as you had no possessions of your own. You kept your pyjamas under your pillow. The windows had no curtains but they had blinds for the wartime blackout which were screwed into place (Laing and McQuarrie, 1989).

The post Second World War Period saw a rapid expansion in mental illness services leading to the 1959 Mental Health Act. More out-patient facilities reduced the stigma and helped earlier treatment. The development of the NHS helped expand and give increasing power to the profession of psychiatry. The National Association for Mental Health (later called MIND), an increasingly powerful lobby for mental illness interests, was founded out of the amalgamation of three national voluntary bodies in the 1940s.

In 1948, John Vincent wrote about his experiences in leaving a lunatic asylum:

What of those who do leave the asylum? They will forever bear a stigma. They will be regarded with suspicion by workmates and even by loving relatives. Prospective employers will shake their heads as the gap on the record is explained. I myself have suffered. It has been a cruel disappointment to discover that even dignitaries of the Christian Church share the common notions about mental disease. It is most urgently necessary that the public should be educated to understand and sympathise with mental disorders. (Vincent, 1948, p. 18)

The only study in the 1950s on public attitudes towards mental illness was Carstairs and Wing's analysis of the BBC radio programme *The Hurt Mind* (Ramon, 1985, p. 134). Twenty-five thousand letters were received in 1957, which indicates considerable concern. In the next year, *Plea for the Silent* was edited by two MPs (Johnson and Dodds, 1958). This book was mainly a collection of patients' reports criticising psychiatrists, duly authorised officers and nurses who are accused of a dehumanising approach, excessive use of force, neglect of basic citizens' rights, lack of respect for patients and little attempt at genuine communication.

The last thirty years has seen a tremendous explosion in accounts about the experience of mental illness and treatment. These come from six main sources. The most commonly published are *case studies*, written by mental illness professionals mainly to illustrate their diagnosis and treatment. For example, D. E. Smith describes how 'K' comes to be defined by her friends as mentally ill and what that means to her and them (D. E. Smith, 1978). More traditionally, J. Hopkins describes twenty months of psychotherapy with an eight-year-old boy (Hopkins, 1977). David Malan's important book on psychotherapy is a large sandwich of theoretical material and case examples (Malan, 1979). Much less common are case studies written conjointly by professionals and clients/patients. 'Singer or Song' is a study by a professional social worker and a person with suicidal tendencies (Ford and Hollick, 1979).

A more recent development is literature by *pseudo-patients*. These are people, mainly mental illness professionals, who deliberately get themselves shut away in mental hospitals. In the best known, by Rosenhan, eight pseudo-patients were admitted to twelve assorted hospitals in the USA. Their day-to-day behaviour on the wards was seen in terms of various pathological conditions. One person taking notes for the study was described in the nursing file as 'engaging in writing behaviour'.

Never were the staff found to assume that one of themselves or the structure of the hospital had anything to do with a patients' behaviour. One psychiatrist pointed to a group of patients who were sitting outside the cafeteria entrance half an hour before lunchtime. To a group of residents (student doctors) he indicated that such behaviour was characteristic of the oral-acquisitive nature of the syndrome. It seemed not to occur to him that there were few things to anticipate in a psychiatric hospital besides eating.

Rosenhan concluded that mental hospitals had rigid hierarchical structures. Patients were made to feel powerless and depersonalised, and there was a heavy reliance on psychotropic drugs. Psychiatric labels were sticky and carried important stigmas which involved practical difficulties both at home and work (Rosenhan, 1973).

Research into *user viewpoints* has also blossomed. In 1967, the famous campaigning book *Sans Everything* looked at the abuse and neglect of psycho-geriatric patients, and was mauled by the medical profession (Robb, 1967). A comprehensive survey of patients' perceptions of mental hospitals was completed by the King's Fund in 1977 and is summarised in Chapter 4.

Studying the views of service users has become a growth industry. There are dozens of publications. For example, the Community Psychiatric Nurses Association published *The Patients Case – Views from Experience: Living Inside and Out of a Psychiatric Hospital* which consists of rather disembodied comments about services (Community Psychiatric Nurses, 1987). My own *Voices of Experience* summarised many sources (Brandon, 1981).

One classic study was by the sociologist Erving Goffman. He concluded wisely:

> Mental patients can find themselves in a special bind. To get out of the hospital, or ease their life within it, they must show acceptance of the place accorded them, and the place accorded them is to support the occupational role of those who appear to force this bargain. This self-alienating moral servitude, which perhaps helps to account for some inmates becoming mentally confused, is achieved by invoking the great tradition of the expert servicing relation, especially its medical variety. Mental patients can find themselves crushed by the weight of a service ideal that eases life for the rest of us. (Goffman, 1968)

Particularly valuable is an American study which argues that the behaviour of people living as 'chronic schizophrenics' in mental hospitals is exceptionally intelligent, very rational and extremely purposive. Their overall purpose is to remain there. They behave insufficiently 'crazy' to avoid the locked ward and just sufficiently disturbed not to be discharged. The study questions the 'victim' role of such patients. They sabotage efforts at rehabilitation and returning them to the community. They make themselves invisible by avoiding contact with psychiatrists and being moderately crazy at the right moments (Braginsky *et al.*, 1969).

There is considerable material by *relatives* of patients. Martha Robinson wrote about her son labelled schizophrenic who took his own life in 1977, after a long and courageous struggle to understand his condition (Robinson, 1979). Ruth Ward wrote about Christmas Day some years previous when her son declared 'I know I am Jesus Christ' (Ward, 1981). Relatives have been a powerful force in forming campaigning groups like the National Schizophrenia Fellowship and SANE.

Material in an indirect form is provided through novels, short stories and films. *Psycho*, *One Flew Over the Cuckoo's Nest*, *The Three Faces of Eve*, *The Snakepit*, *Birdy* are just a few of the many hundreds of films on the popular madness theme. In Bernard Kops's novel *On Margate Sands*, 46-year-old Brian Singleton has just been released from mental hospital after twenty-six years (Kops, 1978).

The American poetess Sylvia Plath wrote the novel *The Bell Jar* (1963) from her own experiences of depression and treatment. She later committed suicide. Her central character is admitted to a mental hospital: 'I focused more closely, trying to pry some clue from their stiff postures. I made out men and women, and boys and girls who must be as young as I, but there was a uniformity to their faces, as if they had lain for a long time on a shelf, out of the sunlight, under siftings of pale, fine dust.' In Jennifer Dawson's novel *The Ha Ha* (1962) Josephine has just been removed from Oxford University to a mental hospital. Most of these films and novels have had a strongly autobiographical feel. Often they were, as with Sylvia Plath, the recycling of the author's personal experiences of mental illness.

The Comforts of Madness, a novel written by a psychiatric nurse which sees the services through the eyes of a catatonic patient, won the Whitbread prize in 1988:

There are both men and women here, and all, save Roger and myself, are quite ancient. They wander incessantly, the women more so than the men, trying locked doors, picking hopeless fights, though many are remarkable agile. The air is impregnated with the constant smell of faeces and urine. Many talk constantly about their mothers, screaming for them sometimes, their voices seeming to come from crazed souls that have already passed on the grave in advance of their crumbly old bodies. (Sayer, 1988)

Last and most important are the direct writings and broadcasts by *patients* themselves. More and more people have continued to come out of the closet in the tradition of John Perceval. Organisations like MIND, the Mental Patients Union, Survivors Speak Out, and the magazine *Asylum* provide a forum for these valuable accounts. *Asylum* argues the case for democratic psychiatry and gives a central place to the arguments of those with direct experiences of the psychiatric services. Many stories from an increasing number of sources tell of epic struggles to recover confidence, to find a richer and less lonely life and to break free from dependence on professional help.

Sutherland's (a Professor of Psychology) book *Breakdown* is still perhaps the best known:

the tedium of the evenings oppressed almost everyone, and the boredom at the weekends afflicted those who did not take weekend leave. We all felt we were very much in the power of the hospital authorities. Although we were free to discharge ourselves at any time, few were in a condition to do so, and so long as one stayed in hospital, one had to agree to the conditions imposed; one woman was forbidden to communicate with her husband even by letter or telephone. This may have been good therapy for her – I never discovered why this condition was imposed – but it made the rest of us uneasy lest we suffered a similar fate. None of us like the constant surveillance, and many of us felt oppressed because we could not deal on equal terms with nurses and doctors; we were mad; they did not need to take us seriously. (Sutherland, 1977)

Janet Cresswell, a patient in Broadmoor maximum security hospital, wrote a play called *The One-Sided Wall*. The play is based on a mental health tribunal where psychiatric patients appear once a year pleading for liberty. 'If a label says mad, then the more you protest, the more they show you have no insight into your madness' (see Brown, 1989).

There have been centuries of experiences of patients of lunacy/ mental illness services. Most of their sparse comments record bad conditions: little and poor-quality food; cruelty or, at best, neglect or little respect and understanding from poorly paid and trained staff; often rejection by close relatives; social and economic marginalisation leading to poverty; the absence of privacy. 'One enamelled national health bed with a couple of square feet of "bed space", a hospital ward with rows of beds separated from each other by barricades of sheets, blankets and lockers erected by their privacy seeking individuals' (Hinshelwood and Manning, 1979). 'Getting up means wearing someone else's clothes. The green woollen dress smells of someone else's sickness. Then you sit in the corridor opposite doors where the screaming comes from' (*MIND OUT*, October 1974). Until this century, only the visionaries and reformers listened to these patients' stories. In the eyes of most others they had spoilt identities – thoroughly discredited witnesses.

Most professionals ignored their evidence except as fodder for an endless stream of case histories. Patients have been squeezed injuriously into an endless series of ideological boxes to demonstrate and illustrate a variety of particular theories. They were hardly ever seen as whole persons.

The net of mental illness has been greatly extended with a vast increase in the numbers of people employed in the industry. A hundred and fifty years ago, the term 'mad' was used mainly to describe those who were compulsorily detained; those perceived as requiring removal and locking-up. Increasingly, society has become less tolerant and the major industrial and social forces have pressed for more effective ways of marginalising those who made little economic contribution. The Chief Medical Officers report (HMSO, 1950) suggested that the 'apparently normal could be mentally ill'. 'We are tending to widen our definition and our recognition of psychological distress' (*Better Services for the Mentally Ill*, HMSO, 1975, p. 2). The lunatic asylum has had a major role in the marginalisation of people in poverty.

Our inheritance is that people have very low expectations of mental illness services. Lonsdale notes that 'The low expectations which both patients and caregivers have of these services could cause low usage of them' (Lonsdale *et al.*, 1980). User surveys must be extremely careful about people's judgement of what is 'satisfactory'. Traditionally people have been 'satisfied' with what would have been regarded as very poor quality services in commerce or catering.

I recall a long-stay patient in Whittingham Hospital, one of the 'scandal' psychiatric hospitals of the 1970s and close to my home, talking with approval about a ward to which he had been moved. 'But what's so good about it?' I asked. 'It's great. It's wonderful. The nurses don't beat you up.'

It is clear that lack of attention to the voices of users persists. Foudraine asks, 'What concerns me most is why we do not see that those who are called "psychotic" or "schizophrenic" can teach us *most* about the human condition; why we have been so unprepared and unwilling to listen especially to them' (Foudraine, 1971, p. 410). Braisby comments:

> in the taxing and confusing process of moving onwards a different pattern of services, the consequences of change for people who are living as patients in the large institutions is something that is very easily lost sight of by professionals. From the psychiatric literature it is clear that little attention has been given to the experiences of patients who have been involved in major changes in services. Yet tens of thousands of people have moved and are currently moving from large hospitals to a variety of living situations in the community. They have a wealth of views and ideas on what has helped and hindered in managing this change. If the shift to community-based psychiatric care is to benefit those living in psychiatric hospitals then some urgent consideration has to be given to patient participation. (Braisby, 1989)

References

John Arlidge, *On the State of Lunacy and the Legal Provision for the Insane* (Churchill, 1859).

Samuel Bakewell, *An Essay on Insanity* (Edinburgh, 1833) p. 47.

Gregory Bateson (ed.), *Perceval's Narrative* (Stanford University Press, 1961).

Edmund Blunden (ed.), *Sketches in the Life of John Clare by Himself* (Cobden-Sanderson, 1931).

B. M. Braginsky *et al.*, *Methods of Madness: The Mental Hospital as a Last Resort* (Holt, 1969).

Don Braisby in David Towell and Tom McAusland, 'Managing Psychiatric Services in Transition: An Overview', section 2, *King's Fund Working Papers* (1989).

David Brandon, *Voices of Experience* (MIND, 1981).

Georgina Brown, 'The Power of Words over Sentences', *The Independent* (1 March 1989).

Robert Burton, *The Anatomy of Melancholy* (Hodson, 1621).

Community Psychiatric Nurses Association, *The Patients Case – Views from Experience: Living Inside and Out of a Psychiatric Hospital* (1987).

John Conolly, *An Inquiry Concerning the Indications of Insanity* (London, 1830) pp. 4–5.

John Conolly, *Treatment of the Insane without Mechanical Restraints* (London, 1856) pp. 102–3.

Jennifer Dawson, *The Ha Ha* (Penguin, 1962).

J. Ford and M. Hollick, 'Singer of the Song – An Autobiographical Account of a Suicidally Destructive Person and her Social Worker', *British Journal of Social Work*, 9(1979) p. 471.

Michel Foucault, *Madness and Civilization* (Tavistock, 1971) p. 70.

Michel Foucault, *Mental Illness and Psychology* (Harper Colophon Books, 1976) pp. 67–8.

Jan Foudraine, *Not Made of Wood* (Quartet Books, 1971) p. 410.

Sander Gilman, *Seeing the Insane* (John Wiley, 1982).

Erving Goffman, *Asylums – Essays on the Social Situation of Mental Patients and Other Inmates* (Penguin, 1968) pp. 335–6.

Mary R. Glover, *The Retreat York – An Early Experiment in the Treatment of Mental Illness* (Sessions, 1984) pp. 48–9.

HMSO, Medical Officers Report, 1950.

HMSO, *Better Services for the Mentally Ill* (1975) p. 2.

Marcia Hamilcar, 'Legally Dead', in Dale Peterson (ed.) *A Mad People's History of Madness* (Univ. of Pittsburgh Press, 1982).

Edward Hare, 'Schizophrenia Before 1800 – The Case of the Rev George Trosse', *Psychological Medicine*, 18(1988) pp. 279–85.

John Haslam, *Illustrations of Madness* (Routledge, 1988) p. xiii, Roy Porter, Introduction.

R. Hinshelwood and Nick Manning (eds), *Therapeutic Communities* (Routledge & Kegan Paul, 1979) p. 56.

J. Hopkins, 'Living under the Threat of Death', *Journal of Child Psychotherapy*, 4(3) (1977) pp. 5–21.

Richard Hunter and Ida MacAlpine, *Three Hundred Years of Psychiatry – 1535–1860* (Oxford Univ. Press, 1963) p. 358.

K. Jaspars, *General Psychopathology* (1923) translated by J. Hoenig and M. W. Hamilton (University of Chicago Press, 1963) p. 425.

D. M. Johnson and N. Dodds (eds) *The Plea for the Silent* (Johnson, 1958).

Kathleen Jones, *Lunacy: Law and Conscience 1744–1845*, edited by W. J. H. Sprott (Routledge & Kegan Paul, 1955) p. 116.

Kathleen Jones, *A History of the Mental Health Services* (Routledge & Kegan Paul, 1972) p. 41.

King's Fund Centre, *Psychiatric Hospitals Viewed by their Patients* (1977).

Bernard Kops, *On Margate Sands* (Secker & Warburg, 1978).

Jimmy Laing and Dermot McQuarrie, *Fifty Years in the System* (Mainstream Publishing, 1989).

Susan Lonsdale *et al.*, *Long Term Psychiatric Patients: A Study in Community Care* (PSSC, 1980).

David H. Malan, *Individual Psychotherapy and the Science of Psychodynamics* (Butterworth, 1979).

Henry Maudsley, *Responsibility in Mental Disease*, 2nd edn (Kegan Paul, 1874).

Henry Maudsley, 'Illustration of a Variety of Insanity', *Journal of Mental Science*, 14(1868) pp. 149–62.

Charles Mercier 'Vice, Crime and Insanity', in *A System of Medicine*, edited by Thomas Clifford Allbutt and Humphrey Davy Rolleston (Macmillan, 1910, 2nd edn).

Urbane Metcalf, 'The Interior of Bethlehem Hospital', in Dale Peterson (ed.), *A Mad People's History of Madness*.

Wilfred Owen, *Collected Works*.

William Parry-Jones, *The Trade in Lunacy* (Routledge & Kegan Paul, 1972) pp. 7–8.

Dale Peterson (ed.), *A Mad People's History of Madness* (Univ. of Pittsburgh Press, 1982) pp. 6–18.

Sylvia Plath, *The Bell Jar* (Heinemann, 1963).

Roy Porter, 'Diary of a Seventeenth Century Madman', in *Lectures on the History of Psychiatry*, edited by R. M. Murray and T. H. Turner (Gaskell, Royal College of Psychiatrists, 1990).

Shulamit Ramon, *Psychiatry in Britain – Meaning and Policy* (Croom Helm, 1985) p. 69.

W. H. J. Rivers, 'Freud's Psychology of the Unconscious', *The Lancet* (16 June 1917).

Barbara Robb, *Sans Everything – A Case to Answer* (Nelson, 1967).

Martha Robinson, 'Schizophrenia – The Hell Within', *Community Care* (12 July 1979).

D. L. Rosenhan, 'On Being Sane in Insane Places', *Science*, 179(1973) pp. 250–8.

Thomas W. Salmon, *The Care and Treatment of Mental Disease and War Neuroses in the British Army* (War Work Committee of the National Committee for Mental Hygiene, 1917 (New York)) p. 31.

Paul Sayer, *The Comforts of Madness* (Constable, 1988) p. 120.

Andrew T. Scull, *Museums of Madness – The Social Organisation of Insanity in Nineteenth Century England* (Penguin, 1982) p. 226.

Elaine Showalter, *The Female Malady – Women, Madness and English Culture – 1830 to 1980* (Virago, 1987) p. 17.

Vieda Skultans, *English Madness: Ideas on Insanity 1580–1890* (Routledge & Kegan Paul, 1979) p. 88.

D. E. Smith, 'K is Mentally Ill: The Anatomy of a Factual Account', *Sociology*, 12(1) (1978) pp. 23–53.

L. D. Smith, 'Behind Closed Doors: Lunatic Asylum Keepers: 1800–60', *Social History of Medicine* vol. 1, no. 13, (December 1988) p. 309.

Stuart Sutherland, *Breakdown* (Paladin, 1977).

J. W. and A. Tibble, *John Clare – A Life* (Cobden-Sanderson, 1932) p. 421.

Samuel Tuke, *A Description of The Retreat* (York, 1813) pp. 133–4.

John Vincent, *Inside the Asylum* (Allen & Unwin, 1948).

John Walton, 'The Treatment of Pauper Lunatics in Victorian England: The Case of the Lancaster Asylum 1816–70', ch. 7 in Andrew Scull (ed.), *Madhouses, Mad-Doctors and Madmen – The Social History of Psychiatry in the Victorian Era* (The Athlone Press, 1981) pp. 191–2.

Ruth Ward, 'Schizophrenia: How One Family Coped', *MIND OUT* (April 1981).

3

Winds and Tides

This chapter tries to make the link between the history of users' experiences and the modern services. The experience of users of mental illness services has apparently become more significant in policy terms. At three levels, various ideas and forces which give that experience prominence have helped create different sorts of services – structural, professional, and users getting together to influence, and sometimes create and run, services.

The mental illness services are swept along by powerful social and economic forces – winds and tides. These are taken for granted by the people who ply their wares on the beach. Some forces are too large and omniscient to see. When I took my two-year-old youngest son to London Zoo, he was unable to see the elephants because they were too large. However, the recently hatched quails were a delight.

Recently, there have been some of the highest unemployment figures since the 1930s. Many former psychiatric patients, who in better years had found unskilled work, are now out of work. A recent report found that only one in five of 500 psychiatric patients had jobs (MIND/Roehampton Institute, 1990).

Evidence shows that unemployed people die earlier, especially by suicide, and suffer more physical and mental ill-health than those in work. In most surveys about a fifth of unemployed people report a deterioration in their mental health since losing their jobs. They suffer more from insomnia, anxiety, depression and irritability; the longer their unemployment lasts, the worse their health gets (Smith, 1985–6). Brenner sketched the overall links between mental illness and unemployment (Brenner, 1973).

Poverty is the major symptom of mental illness. Some of that impoverishment is unnecessary. In a recent study fifty psychiatric patients using day hospitals were interviewed about social security benefits. Of those already receiving social security 25 per cent were entitled to at least one further benefit. Over half the unclaimed benefits were for housing benefit. Local authorities did not provide adequate information to potential claimants. Social workers were not seen as informants about social security (Allen and West, 1989).

Government cutbacks on local authority house building and the sales of existing council houses make reasonably priced accommodation scarce – one reason for the increasing numbers of homeless psychiatric patients. There are innumerable studies connecting homelessness and mental illness. The most recent interviewed 124 men in hostels and diagnosed 31 per cent as schizophrenic (Timms and Fry, 1989).

One hopeful pressure is for the greater involvement of users in both making policy and managing services. Increased choices and greater participation have become popular slogans in areas like education, housing and planning. The Skeffington Report on planning was an important landmark in participation. It argued in 1969 that people should be kept informed about the preparation of a local plan for their area. 'Statements should be published about the timescale of planning and information given to the public.' 'Public meetings should be convened' to discuss relevant issues (HMSO, 1969).

Throughout the 1970s, events such as the setting up of community health councils in the 1974 NHS reorganisation and, all in the same year of 1971, the Seebohm report on Social Services Departments, the Taylor committee on school governing boards, and the Department of the Environment report on housing tenancy, proposed the greater involvement of users, although these were mostly and paradoxically unelected. The Education Reform Act of 1988 gave schools and their management committees more autonomy from local education authorities (Dry, 1990). All these nominated committees and boards effectively excluded the people most in poverty. On the health side, the first Griffiths report (1983) criticised the NHS management for failing to talk effectively to users and staff about how well or badly the service was being delivered at local level. Consumerism was given a major role in the Cumberlege report on community nursing. The Disabled Persons Act (1986) supported these developments by formalising advocacy for people with disabilities but failed to

attract the necessary funding to put into action most of its
ingredients.

A number of local authorities tried to bring bureaucratic services
closer to the citizens who paid for them. Patch, locality and
neighbourhood-based social services were popular in the mid-
1980s (Beresford and Croft, 1986).

> In Islington we have undertaken a total programme of decen-
> tralisation of services. In practical terms this means we have 24
> local neighbourhood offices which offer most of the major
> Council services. The major components of these offices are
> social services and housing. From the clients' point of view the
> neighbourhood office offers a one-stop shop. The Council is now
> in the process of developing active neighbourhood forums made
> up of elected members of the community and local organisations
> who will, in the long term, have an increasing say in how services
> are delivered in that area and contribute to the overall policy
> making process. (Devenney, 1988)

Perhaps the people with the least say are the people in poverty who
used those services.

The World Health Organisation (WHO) Alma-Ata declaration
states: 'The people have the right and duty to participate
individually and collectively in the planning and implementation
of their health care' (WHO, 1978). Another WHO document states
that '. . . representative community participation should be the
rule in all official bodies that deal with . . . health', and more
specifically, 'Care should be taken to include representatives both
from vulnerable groups and from groups that have shown
particular interest and initiative in improving the health of
communities' (WHO, 1985). The White Paper on the NHS,
Working for Patients reminds us that 'the patient's needs will
always be paramount' (HMSO, 1988).

The Wagner Report on residential services joined this extensive
refrain. It outlined the goals of staff development and training
policy: 'an ethos in which the needs and interests of the residents
are paramount. This in turn requires the staff to be consistently
seeking to change and adapt their own responses to the changing
and varied needs of the residents.' It recommended that:

A statutory duty should be placed on local authorities to propose a reasonable package of services, enabling a person to remain in their own home if that is their choice and it is reasonable for them to do so . . . It is clearly one of the major principles of good residential practice that residents should have as much control over their own lives as possible, maintaining normal lifestyles and exercising choice. In particular, it is our view that residents are entitled to be involved in all decisions which affect their daily lives. (Wagner, 1988)

Participation in mental illness services was first proposed by central government in the DHSS Draft Circular (1986). It recognised that service users had an essential contribution to make in service planning. 'Planning should be directed towards meeting the needs of individual patients and clients . . . Service providers, clients, their families and community representatives including those of ethnic minorities are to have the opportunity to make a contribution to planning, ensuring the plans are seen by consumers.'

The Short report on mental illness/mental handicap services dampened down any undue enthusiasm and brought us back to the autocratic present:

We have had difficulty in hearing the authentic voice of the ultimate consumers of community care. There have been considerable advances in techniques designed to enable and encourage mentally ill or handicapped people to speak for themselves . . . But there is a long way to go. Services are still mainly designed by providers and not users, whether families or clients, and in response to blue prints rather than in answer to demands. Matching the service to the consumer rather than vice versa should be the one central aim of community care in the future. (Short Report, 1984–5).

Much more was written about participation than practised. Much space was spent extolling the virtues of participation by users with little practical guidance as to how it might be achieved.

The community care paper by the influential Royal College of Psychiatrists includes no direct mention of user participation.

Anderson argues that:

> the psychiatric profession must learn more about the scope and
> utility of user participation and encourage it: the persistence of
> patients' groups seems to underlie many of the most innovative
> programmes in mental health care. This could improve clinical
> outcome, encourage agreement about priorities in treatment, and
> resolve an embarrassing divergence between providers and users
> of services. (Anderson, 1989).

Mental illness policy since the war, has been dominated by the
'community care' debate. Originally these were policies about
wards in the community, tracing back to the Royal Commission
on Mental Illness and Mental Deficiency of 1954–7 which
examined the problems of the outdated mental hospitals and
recommended the 'development of community care' as a duty of
local authorities. It is only very recently that people have tried to
turn the community care discussions into debates about user
influence and control.

Enoch Powell, then Minister of Health, in a watershed speech at
the 1961 National Association for Mental Health (later changed to
MIND) conference described the mental hospitals as:

> isolated, majestic, imperious, brooded over by gigantic water
> tower and chimney combined rising unmistakable and daunting
> out of the countryside . . . I have intimated to the hospital
> authorities who will be producing the constituent elements of the
> national hospital plan that in fifteen years time there may well be
> needed not more than half as many places in hospitals for mental
> illness as there are today. Expressed in numerical terms, this
> would represent a redundancy of no fewer than 75,000 beds.

By 1976, the rundown was roughly on target with only 76,000
psychiatric hospital beds left but there had been little attempt to
construct alternative systems in the community.

The DHSS noted in 1981: 'Most people who need long term care
can and should be looked after in the community. This is what
most of them want for themselves and those responsible for their
care believe to be best. There are many people in hospital who

would not need to be there if appropriate community services were available' (DHSS, 1981).

The Short Report stated: 'The committee supports a policy for community care for mentally disabled people which cannot be drawn up over night nor on the cheap.' It defined the basic principle, none too optimistically, as: 'Appropriate care should be provided for individuals in such a way as to enable them to lead as normal an existence as possible given their particular disabilities and to minimise disruption of life within their community' (Short Report, 1984–5). Normality was now an important yardstick.

In the last decade, the drive towards 'consumerist' services has been inspired by market economics. An interest in the techniques of commercial enterprise is now widespread among public sector managers. It is very much in tune with the ideas underpinning the 'enterprise culture'. Central to those ideas is the notion that there should be a substantial reduction in the role of the state and an increase in choice (Winn and Quick, 1989). To choose freely, it is necessary to have options and relevant resources. Many suspect that market metaphors are simply a cover for extensive cost-cutting or a device to offer increasing choice to those who can pay out of their own pocket.

The Government White Paper *Caring for People* pushes the case for a mixed economy. It wants local authorities to take a lead in planning, co-ordinating and monitoring services but to make less direct provision. A greater proportion of services would come from the private sector. It recommended three fundamental objectives:

* to enable people to live as normal a life as possible in their own homes or in a homely environment in the local community;
* to provide the right amount of care and support to help people achieve maximum possible independence and, by acquiring or reacquiring basic living skills, help them to achieve their full potential;
* to give people a greater individual say in how they live their lives and the services they need to help them to do so. (HMSO, 1989)

Again there is stress on 'normal' and 'homely' and helping people to achieve 'their full potential'. Community care now means not only living in an ordinary neighbourhood but giving 'people a greater individual say in how they live their lives'.

Changes in mental illness services need vast changes in public attitudes; in the conservatism of relatives and other 'carers'; in socio-economic strategies – for example existing funding systems encourage institutionalised services; in a much higher political priority. I have chosen to look at the ways in which users experiences are having an impact on three levels: on organisational structures; on the way professionals think and practise; on an increased consciousness and assertiveness among users.

How are organisations to achieve increased individualisation in congregated systems which tend towards block treatment – treating people as if similiar? There have been attempts to individualise large services through both quality assurance work and the more recent innovation, largely imported from the USA – case management.

One proponent of quality assurance argues for three routes towards quality assurance in a health authority. There should be direct accountability which asks appropriate questions about quality, provides relevant information and implements agreed solutions. Indirect accountability means delegating responsibility for monitoring technical quality to professional groups. 'Lay managers are not qualified to make technical judgements but they can ask that someone else does.' Groups like the Health Advisory Service, the National Development Team . . . can provide external accountability (Shaw, 1986) .

Helen Smith considered the safeguarding of quality in long-stay psychiatric hospitals (Smith, 1989). The Working Group which produced the study considered two basic questions: 'How do we know what a high quality service looks like for residents? How can we bring about positive changes in the working practices?' It recommended the setting-up of Quality Action Groups to implement and monitor the work towards five major principles:

* People in longstay wards have the same human values as others and have a right to respect and privacy
* A person has a right to an individual plan . . .
* A service should seek to ensure that people participate as fully as possible in the local community
* A person has a right to sufficient and individualised support...

* People in longstay wards have the right to expect that a positive image of residents will always be projected within and outside of the hospital . . .

These are splendid principles but strangely absent is any participation in the hospital ward. Democracy begins at the hospital exit! How can patients fully participate in the local community if there is no democracy on the ward?

Case management attempts to individualise large services (King, 1990). 'Case management is a tool used to connect a client from a particular group with all the services he or she requires in a situation where service provision is complex.' It was imported from the USA to increase user choices, minimise confusion in the provision of services, tackle the problems of ill-co-ordinated and overlapping services resulting in people 'falling through the net'.

A pioneering project in Camden and Islington – Choice – dealt with people who had a physical disability. Between May 1986 and September 1987 142 people were referred for case management. They each received a holistic assessment as well as co-ordination and access to services. When a service was not readily available, the Case Manager acted as the client's representative or encouraged self advocacy. Case management has benefits on three levels: easy access for clients; service providers benefit by receiving a specialist planning and co-ordination service; policy-makers gain because the Case Manager is uniquely placed to feed back about needs and gaps in resources (Banks, 1989).

The challenge for effective case management is to help provide genuine options for clients. Beardshaw and Towell ask how these options can be achieved. 'How should case managers be held accountable to their agency and to their clients?' and will 'clients and carers be allowed to 'opt out' of case management organised by social services authorities and provide their own?' (Beardshaw and Towell, 1990).

The government White Paper *Caring for People* seems to give an enormous boost to case management systems, particularly those with some kind of 'contract' between the users and the service providers. Elements like the expected nature and quality of the service can be defined. Such 'contracts' only really have force if the user has power and alternatives – to which any regular British Rail traveller can testify!

There have been many major influences on the mental illness professions over the last twenty years. One important challenge was that of the 'therapeutic community', pioneered by Dr Maxwell Jones. 'The eminent figure of Maxwell Jones sought to retain the asylum, but to transform it into a genuinely therapeutic and curative establishment' (Miller, 1986). From his pioneering work at the Henderson Hospital in south London and Dingleton Hospital, near Melrose in Scotland, Jones diagnosed:

> We still know far too little about the process of becoming ill, but there is now a growing awareness in psychiatry that, if proper attention is paid to the persons and situations with which the patient is in contact, he may be given an opportunity to take up social roles which can enhance his capacity to remain well. 'Becoming ill' usually means the appearance of symptoms, and the psychiatrist in the past has been preoccupied with these symptoms and with the problems of grouping and classifying them as disease entities. But it now seems, in some cases at least, that becoming ill, or assuming the role of patient, may be the last resort of an individual who lacks adequate social support and is unable to do anything to help himself. (Jones, 1968, p. 13)

At least part of the remedy lay in

> ward meetings, living–learning situations and a general therapeutic culture may constitute a form of therapy. At the very least we are attempting to understand and plan for patient management, in a way which will enhance the effectiveness of any of the more specific treatment methods. But over and above this, we believe that by harnessing and directing certain forces in the social environment a new dimension of treatment may emerge. (ibid, p. 115)

Staff and patients were jointly charged with responsibility for the therapeutic process.

One way to demonstrate social learning in a mental hospital is to have a review immediately following a daily ward meeting involving all patients and staff on a ward. Discussion of the problems of living and human relationships in the ward meeting are witnessed by everyone, but viewed differently by each individual according to many variables, including personality, educational background, motivation, etc. . . . To turn this shared experience into a learning situation (training) for the staff, a review supervised by a competent facilitator has enormous potential for social learning. (Jones, 1968, p. 135)

The professional was still conducting the orchestra.

'Familiar practices include freeing of communications, flattening of the authority pyramid, sharing of responsibility, decision-making by consensus, analysis of events, provision of living–learning opportunities, and examination of roles and role-relationships . . . Throughout the world the liberalization of mental hospitals owes much to this approach' (Morrice in Hinshelwood and Manning, 1979).

The therapeutic community movement was a serious attempt to respect patients' social situation and retain the large mental hospital functions. It was doomed to failure because politics and therapy were hopelessly entangled and professionals held on to dominant roles. The influence of Maxwell Jones has waned considerably since the 1970s. Little direct impact remains except within the Richmond Fellowship national network of local community hostels.

An even larger psychiatric comet was Anti-psychiatry. It was fundamentally critical of clinical approaches to people and of the assumed physical causes of mental distress. It argued that this distress was a reflection of the psychological discomfort and suffering rooted in family relationships, leading to the untenable position of one family member, which mirrored the society in which we live – its violence and contradictions. It argued that so-called madness was intelligible. The 'patient' and his/her experiences should be taken seriously and respected.

Psychiatry could be, and some psychiatrists are, on the side of transcendence, of genuine freedom, and of human growth. But psychiatry can so easily be a technique of brain washing, of inducing behaviour that is adjusted, by (preferably) non-injurious torture. In the best places, where strait-jackets are abolished, doors are unlocked, leucotomies largely forgone, these can be replaced by more subtle lobotomies and tranquillizers that place the bars of Bedlam and the locked doors inside the patient. (Laing, 1961)

Schatzman wrote:

Mental hospitals like prison confine deviant persons, but they confuse their inmates more, since they do not tell them what rules they have broken, nor even that they have broken rules. The psychiatrist in the mental hospital tries to persuade himself, his colleagues in the medical profession, the staff, the 'patients', the patients' families and friends, and society that he practises medicine, and denies to himself and others that any persuasion occurs or is even necessary. To frame his activities within a medical model he calls a trial, 'examination'; a judgement 'a diagnosis'; a sentence, 'disposition'; and correction, 'treatment'. If his 'patients' claim they are not ill they challenge his pretensions. (Schatzman, 1971)

Anti-psychiatry was a loose and woolly label to describe psychiatrists like Laing and Cooper, pioneering ways of accepting the consumers as an intelligible human being, no matter how 'mad'. They developed residential communities like the Arbours Center and the Philadelphia Association and re-cast therapeutic ways of working with people and reduced social distances between professionals and consumers. The anti-psychiatrists had an extensive international influence, but that has waned considerably. This movement never had a secure British base – many workers came from overseas – and now only a few service fragments remain.

Another later influence was De-professionalism. This was based on a deep rooted scepticism about all trained elites, often socially and geographically distant and receiving high salaries. Illich comments: 'The age of professionals will be remembered as the time when politics withered, when voters, guided by professors, entrusted to technocrats the power to legislate needs, renounced the authority to decide who needs what and suffered monopolistic oligarchies to determine the means by which these needs shall be met' (Illich *et al.*, 1977).

Man's consciously lived fragility, individuality and relatedness make the experience of pain, of sickness and of death an integral part of his life. The ability to cope with this trio autonomously is fundamental to his health. As he becomes dependent on the management of his intimacy, he renounces his autonomy and his health *must* decline. The true miracle of modern medicine is diabolical. It consists not only of making individuals but whole populations survive on inhumanly low levels of personal health. That health should decline with increasing health service delivery is unforeseen only by the health managers, precisely because their strategies are the result of their blindness to the inalienability of life. (Illich, 1975)

Illich and followers inspired many to re-think their professionalism and learn greater humility. In the psychiatric field, who were we serving and with what means and to what ends? Those questions still reverberate with no easy answers particularly in the areas of counselling and psychotherapy. Are we helping or hindering? (Brandon, 1976/1990)

A more recent influence is Normalisation, largely developed by Wolfensberger in the USA in the early 1970s, from work originating in Denmark and Norway. It was later re-named 'social role valorisation'. His definition was 'The use of culturally valued means in order to enable people to live culturally valued lives' (Wolfensberger, 1972). He examined how services further devalued their negatively labelled 'clients'. He saw professionals submerged in a general social process to view consumers as less than fully human, colluding with poor quality segregated systems which keep people in abject poverty. Improvement is achieved partly through changing services and professions and partly by increasing the perceived social value of people with handicaps.

The principle of normalisation suggests that human services have an enormous capacity for destructiveness. Service providers set out with a series of principles and are diverted by a forest of hidden agendas, powerful vested interests and unconscious drives. That results in the ideological model of services becoming completely inconsistent with what users and staff actually experience and what they want and need.

McCord argues for increased awareness:

The normalisation principle asserts that agencies will more effectively 'help' people when they recognise the impact of societal perceptions of deviance on human service delivery, and subsequently create services which reduce, rather than magnify, the deviant status of clients. Thus, the normalisation principle urges the development of service systems which . . . attempt to accomplish two things: (1) change the perceptions or values of the perceiver and (2) minimise the stigma of deviancy that activates the perceiver's devaluation. (McCord, 1982)

Normalisation has already had a profound impact on services for people with learning difficulties. Many hundreds of professionals have been on five day Program Analysis of Service Systems (PASS) training courses, the main route into understanding (Race, 1987). Progress in the mental illness field, where the need is even greater, is much slower.

The practical pioneers of this approach are the Harpurhey resettlement team in north Manchester. Their resettlement work of long-stay patients is based on five basic normalisation principles. People should live in ordinary houses. These houses should be dispersed around in the neighbourhood. The main criteria for resettlement should be that people wish to leave hospital. Specialist psychiatric services should be avoided and ordinary facilities explored. Assessment should try to establish what people's needs and wants are and develop a service which meets them (Harpurhey, 1989).

The advocacy movement has struggled for survival over the last decade. MIND pioneered campaigns for the rights of mental illness patients in the early 1970s and was vigorously attacked, particularly by psychiatry, for bringing rights issues into mental illness. It tried to establish clear principles about the nature of citizenship, particularly for those detained under sections of the 1959 Mental Health Act. Its advocacy imprint is seen clearly in the successor Act of 1983. Advocacy initially meant action by professionals, particularly lawyers and has widened out latterly to involve volunteers.

The advocacy/representation movement defines and fights for devalued people's rights. Gostin, the arch exponent of this approach wrote: 'Noble intentions are simply hollow verbiage if the depressed and mentally handicapped persons in the back wards of our hospitals, or forgotten in the community, are unaware of their rights or too passive or powerless to enforce them. "Rights" are meaningless unless they help achieve a better quality of life and dignity for these people' (Gostin, 1983).

The most heartening recent developments have taken place at the level of users and their dialogues with professionals. Major movements like women's mental health, black consciousness of psychiatric oppression, self-help groups and consumerism have begun to impact on the margins of services. Feminists note the disproportionate numbers of women coming into psychiatric treatment:

> Our experience of the world differs radically from men's, and nowhere is this more apparent than in the traditional role models society has established for each sex. The stereotype of femininity – albeit one which is increasingly challenged – focuses on passivity, weakness and dependency. The masculine stereotype on the other hand emphasises competence, activity, analytical ability and independence, all desirable and above all *adult* attributes. Stereotypically feminine characteristics are at odds with accepted notions of adulthood and maturity, and the contradictions this creates for us are parallelled in the mental health services where restrictive definitions of what is 'normal' are not only reinforced by psychiatric treatment but also held up as the ideal. (Women in MIND, 1986)

> we learned that diagnostic labels vary by sex; women are deemed depressed, hysterical, anxiety neurotics, and phobic, whereas men are deemed alcoholic, organic and antisocial. (Brodsky, 1981)

Psychiatry is perceived as an important enemy based largely on male dominated values:

> Psychiatry uses its formulation to maintain the psychiatric version of reality and to play its part in organising and administering the segments of society, as well as seeking to serve the patient population. By doing so it obscures the possibility of understanding the actualisation of certain people's lives in ways other than those offered by psychiatry. Thus it defuses the possibility of other actions or solutions to

peoples differences. We have seen that this is doubly effective for women who do not have the chance to represent their own experiences in the male world . . . Psychiatry has gone hand in hand with the rest of the medical profession, not only in supporting existing views of women but in providing an even more comprehensive ideology to institutionalise their oppression as an inevitable 'fact of life', and in developing practices that both reflect and enforce that oppression. (Penfold and Walker, 1984)

Several studies look at those biases in counselling and psycho-therapy. Broverman examined the attitudes of seventy-nine clinicians of both sexes towards gender differences:

The clinicians' concepts of a healthy mature man do not differ significantly from their concepts of a healthy adult. However, the clinicians' concepts of a healthy, mature woman do differ significantly from their adult health concepts. Clinicians are significantly less likely to attribute traits that characterise healthy adults to a woman than they are likely to attribute those traits to a healthy man.

He explains that

more likely the double standard of health for men and women stems from the clinicians' acceptance of an 'adjustment' notion of health, for example, health consists of a good adjustment to one's environment. In our society men and women are system-atically trained, practically from birth on, to fulfil different social roles. An adjustment notion of health, plus the existence of different norms of male and female behaviour in our society, automatically leads to a double standard of health. Thus for a woman to be healthy from an adjustment viewpoint, she must adjust to and accept the behavioural norms for her sex, even though these behaviours are generally less socially desirable and considered to be less healthy for the generalized competent, mature adult. (Broverman *et al.*, 1981)

One positive development is in the growth of womens self help groups.

The consciousness raising groups which have been the corner-
stone of the women's movement for two decades have success-
fully challenged established attitudes and stereotypes. What were
previously seen as individual problems and failures have been
shown to be the consequences of the contradictory demands
society imposes on women. The women's health movement has
focused attention on the control exerted by a predominantly
male medical profession on women's health, and the way in
which socially-caused illnesses are managed individually. A
direct result of women's increasing politicisation has been the
formation of groups organised along anti-bureaucratic collectiv-
ist and support lines.' (Women in MIND, 1986 p. 92)

'Womankind' was set up in Bristol in 1985 and promotes mental
health in women.

It is a multi-racial project which aims to confront racism,
oppressive stereotypes and prejudices of all kinds . . . The first
open meeting of Women and Mental Health in 1984 brought
together well over 50 women, and the impetus grew from there.
Monthly meetings were held in different parts of Bristol; a day
workshop attended by a 100 women provided by a forum where
experiences of women working in the mental health services and
women who had been helped or hindered by the mental health
system were shared. (Women in MIND, 1986)

Black people also make fundamental criticisms about current
psychiatric ideologies and practices: 'the question of race was not
simply another discrete demographic factor that could be understood within a medical theory of cause and effect but one that
touched on and reawakened doubts about psychiatry's function
and role within our society.' (Francis *et al.*, 1989). Sayal notes:

Historically, there has been a tendency to view black people as
'sick', whether physically (black skin was said to be a form of
leprosy) or mentally (runaway slaves were diagnosed as being
mentally diseased: 'drapetomania' was an incurable urge to run
away). While in Britain the proportion of black people is four
per cent, 25 per cent of patients on psychiatric wards are black.
Today we see the formulation of black-specific mental illnesses.

For example, 'West Indian psychosis', 'paranoia', 'religious mania', even the 'New X psychosis'. Or there is the 'marital psychosis' in Asian women. Black people receive more physical treatments, more and longer ECT and more injected drugs at high dosages. In such physically invasive therapies, the 'side effects' can be lasting. (Sayal, 1990)

The Manchester Afro-Caribbean mental health project estimates that its own community accounts for about 6 per cent of the population but its number of psychiatric patients is usually about 25 per cent. (Afro-Caribbean Mental Health Group, 1990)
Littlewood and Lipsedge comment:

When looking at another group there is always a tendency to relate psychological differences to our own criteria of normality. We have seen that Doctors frequently regard as pathological some experiences such as religious possession which are common in other communities . . . Psychiatry continually reinforces this flawed identity by its concern with the individual rather than the social and by its readiness to accept as primary the reflections thrown into it by other social phenomena. (Littlewood and Lipsedge, 1982)

A considerable network of black mental illness groups has developed. For example, Nafsiyat, a community-based intercultural therapy centre began in London in 1983 to provide psychotherapy for people from ethnic and cultural minority backgrounds.

Nafsiyat challenges many of the preconceptions which have been traditionally associated with 'psychotherapy' and 'trans-cultural psychiatry': that ethnic and cultural minorities are unsuitable for therapy, that payment is always necessary for successful therapy; that it requires long term commitment with frequent attendance. It also requires workers to re-examine their own definition of cultural and racial issues as well as their personal way of working. (Acharyya *et al.*, 1989)

Kingsbury Manor mental health day centre is for Asians in the London Borough of Brent. It has three aims: to provide structured rehabilitation programmes to help in practical daily living; to prevent mental illness relapses through counselling and family support; to provide community education through seminars, articles in local newspapers and training of relevant professionals.

Both black and white groups have taken services into their own hands through self help groups, largely desperately short of money. As early as 1845, Perceval formed 'The Alleged Lunatics Friends Society' to 'stir up an intelligent and active sympathy, on behalf of the most wretched, the most oppressed, the . . . helpless of mankind, by proving with how much needless tyranny they are treated – and this in mockery – by men who pretend indeed their cure, but who are in reality, their tormentors and destroyers.' Perceval saw the problems as primarily political. Powerful people were oppressing those who were vulnerable under a cloak of treatment and care.

In this century, self help groups have varied considerably in their attitudes towards professionals. Some are hostile, others work as partners and colleagues. Based on research into self-help groups in Liverpool, Campion notes that 'Medical education is still failing to prepare doctors for inter-professional teamwork let alone for the more problematic area of community participation in health care. Undoubtedly, the hostility towards the medical profession exhibited by a handful of groups in this study reflects arrogance by some doctors towards the problems of these sufferers' (Campion *et al.*, 1988)

The formidable American consumer movement grew from concerns about service quality and the scarcity of accurate and impartial information. Most real innovation comes from users, as good commercial companies appreciate:

> The excellent companies are the better listeners. They get benefit from client closeness and most of their real innovation comes fron their clients . . . Successful firms pay more attention to their customer than do failures. Successful innovators innovate in response to customer needs, involve potential users in the development of the innovation and understand user needs better. (Peters and Waterman, 1983)

These principles are difficult in mental illness services because of the immense problems in defining a 'good' service. People are not commodities to be bought and sold at the highest possible profit.

How can I tell whether a consultant psychiatrist or social worker
gives me a good service? Is the judgement about whether ECT is
given safely or given at all? Psychiatrists, with their dominant
power, have been able to establish 'no go' areas of 'clinical
judgement' which lay people are supposedly unable to compre-
hend.

Klein outlines some fundamental dilemmas (Klein in Maxwell
and Weaver, 1984, pp. 17–21):

At the heart of the debate about participation, and about the
relationship between the providers and consumers of health care,
there lies a profound contradiction. This is that while the
National Health Service was set up to democratise access to
health care, it is also a monument to the values of enlightened
paternalism. If the overriding policy aim in designing the NHS
was to make sure that everyone should have equal access to the
wonders of medical science, the institutional means reflected the
belief that this could only be brought about by creating more
scope for professional expertise and bureaucratic rationality.
    . . . the health care market is a peculiar one. In particular, it is
characterised by an imbalance of knowledge between consumers
and providers. The consumer does not necessarily know best
(though he or she may do so more often than is assumed by the
professionals). Similarly, mistakes – once made – may often be
irreversible. A defective car can be returned to the garage; a
defective operation poses rather more difficult and perhaps
permanent problems . . . What may be the best buy for the
individual may not necessarily be the best buy for the community collectively: maximising the health of the community as a
whole may actually involve giving individuals less than the
optimum possible treatment, and possibly even denying them
treatment.

How much do all these influences – structural, professional,
userist – add up to real change? I sympathise with Beardshaw's
frustrations:

Much of the fashionable rhetoric about integration is hot air.
Disabled people remain a marginalised and stigmatised
group . . . nevertheless, rhetoric has a certain power. It has

begun to change social attitudes. It is not quite as easy to see disabled people as passive recipients of care . . . But it does not all come down to resources. Many disabled people find unhelpful professional attitudes equally obstructive. Some have come to see health professionals' traditional 'caring' approach as oppressive and patronising. They experience problems of communication, and rigid approaches to treatment that fail to adapt interventions to individual needs. (Beardshaw, 1988)

More specifically, much of the vaunted change in mental illness services has been the discharge of patients out of the poverty stricken environments of the mental hospitals into the prisons, the gutters and the worst council housing estates. Scull notes, 'the primary value of that rhetoric . . . seems to have been the usefulness as ideological camouflage, allowing economy to masquerade as benevolence and neglect as tolerance . . . the alternative to the institution has been to be herded into newly emerging "deviant ghettos", sewers of human misery' (Scull, 1984).

Warner echoes those sentiments:

More than three decades after the onset of deinstitutionalization in the United States, large numbers of the severely mentally ill receive little or no psychiatric treatment. Many are homeless or in jail, others are housed in boarding homes and nursing homes in conditions scarcely better (if at all) than the back wards of the old state hospitals. Why has this happened? A comparison of deinstitutionalization in different Western nations suggests that the process was stimulated by the opportunity for cost savings created by the introduction of disability pensions and, in some countries, by the post war demand for labour. Where labour was in short supply, genuinely rehabilitative programs were developed. When cost saving was the principal motivation, community treatment efforts were weak. In the United States, the tendency to reduce mental hospital beds with minimal community planning was exaggerated by the zeal with which state legislators embraced the opportunity to pass expenses along to the federal government. Contrary to widespread opinion in American psychiatry, the shift to the community does not appear to have been primarily a response to the introduction of anti-psychotic drugs. (Warner, 1989)

References

Sourangshu Acharyya *et al.*, 'Nafsiyat: A Psychotherapy Centre for Ethnic Minorities', *Psychiatric Bulletin*, 13(1989) pp. 358–60.

Afro-Caribbean Mental Health Group, *Newsletter No 2* (Moss Side Health Centre, Monton Street, Moss Side, Manchester M14 4GP, 1990).

Daniel S. Allen and Renate West, 'The Uptake of Social Security Benefits Among Psychiatric Day Hospital Patients', *Psychiatric Bulletin*, 13(1989) pp. 626–7.

Jeremy Anderson, 'Patient Power in Mental Health', *British Medical Journal*, vol 299 (16 December 1989) pp. 1477–8.

Penny Banks, 'The Choice Model of Case Management', *CHOICE*, 1989.

Virginia Beardshaw, 'Aiming to be less of a Client, More of an Ally', *The Health Service Journal* (1 September 1988) pp. 994–6.

Virginia Beardshaw and David Towell, *Assessment and Case Management* (King's Fund Institute, 1990).

John R. Belcher, 'Are Jails Replacing the Mental Health System for the Homeless Mentally Ill?', *Community Mental Health Journal*, vol. 24, no. 3 (Autumn 1988).

Peter Beresford and Suzy Croft, *Whose Welfare: Private Care or Public Services?*, (Lewis Cohen Urban Studies, Brighton Polytechnic, 1986).

David Brandon, *Zen in the Art of Helping* (Routledge & Kegan Paul, 1976; and Penguin, 1990).

Althea and David Brandon, *Putting People First* (Good Impressions, 1988).

M. H. Brenner, *Mental Illness and the Economy* (Harvard University Press, 1973).

Annette M. Brodsky, 'A Decade of Feminist Influence on Psychotherapy', in Elizabeth Howell and Marjorie Bayes (eds), *Women and Mental Health* (Basic Books, 1981).

Inge K. Broverman *et al.*, 'Sex Role Stereotypes and Clinical judgements of Mental Health', in Elizabeth Howell and Marjorie Bayes (eds), *Women and Mental Health* (Basic Books, 1981).

Peter Campion *et al.*, 'Self-Help in Primary Care: Preliminary Findings of a Study in Liverpool', *Journal of the Royal College of General Practitioners* (October 1988) pp. 453–6.

Judi Chamberlin, *On our Own – A Compelling Case for Patient Controlled Services: A Real Alternative to the Institutions that Destroy the Confident Independence of So Many* (MIND, 1988).

DHSS, *Care in Action* (HMSO, 1981).

DHSS, 'Collaboration between the NHS, Local Government and Voluntary Organisations: Joint Planning and Collaboration', Draft Circular (January 1986).

Mike Devenney, 'Consumer-Led services: Fashionable Dogma or Practical Necessity?', in *Hearing the Voice of the Consumer*, Ian White *et al.* (PSI, 1988).

Arnold Dry, 'A Hard Act to Follow', *Community Care* (31 May 1990).

Errol Francis *et al.*, 'Black People and Psychiatry in the U.K.', *Psychiatric Bulletin* 13(1989) pp. 482–5.

Paulo Freire, *Pedagogy of the Oppressed* (Penguin, 1972).

Larry Gostin, *A Practical Guide to Mental Health Law* (MIND, 1983).

HMSO, 'Working for Patients' (1988).

HMSO, *Caring for People: Community Care in the Next Decade and Beyond* (1989).

Harpurhey Resettlement Team: Report 1989.

Ivan Illich, *Medical Nemesis* (Calder & Boyars, 1975).

Ivan Illich, *Celebration of Awareness* (Marion Boyars, 1971).

Ivan Illich *et al.*, *The Disabling Professions* (Marion Boyars, 1977).

Maxwell Jones, *Social Psychiatry in Practice – The Idea of the Therapeutic Community* (Pelican, 1968).

Maxwell Jones, *The Process of Change* (Routledge & Kegan Paul, 1982).

Jane King, 'A Helping Hand', *Community Care* (22 February 1990).

Kingsbury Manor Mental Health Day Centre, 'Aims and Resources' (unpublished, Roe Green Park, 288 Kingsbury Road, London NW9, 1989).

R. D. Laing, *The Divided Self* (Penguin, 1961).

Roland Littlewood and Maurice Lipsedge, *Aliens and Alienists – Ethnic Minorities and Psychiatry* (Pelican, 1982).

Robert Maxwell and Nigel Weaver (eds), *Public Participation in Health* (King Edward's Hospital Fund, 1984).

W. T. McCord, 'From Theory to Reality', *Mental Retardation* vol. 20, no. 6 (American Association on Mental Deficiency, December 1982) pp. 247–53.

Barbara Miller, 'Making Sense of Resource Managment', *Nursing Times* (15 March 1989).

Peter Miller, 'Critical Sociologies of Madness', in *The Power of Psychiatry*, eds Peter Miller and Nikolas Rose (Polity Press, 1986).

MIND/Roehampton Institute, *People First* (1990).

J. K. W. Morrice, 'Basic Concepts: A Critical Review', in R. D. Hinshelwood and Nick Manning (eds), *Therapeutic Communities* (Routledge & Kegan Paul, 1979).

P. Susan Penfold and Gillian A. Walker, *Women and the Psychiatric Paradox* (Open University, 1984).

T. J. Peters and R. H. Waterman, *In Search of Excellence: Lessons from America's Best-Run Companies* (Harper & Row, 1983).

David Race, 'Normalisation: Theory and Practice', in Nigel Malin (ed.), 'Reassessing Community Care' (Croom Helm, 1987).

Anuradha Sayal, 'Black Women and Mental Health', *The Psychologist* (January 1990).

Morton Schatzman, 'Madness and Morals', in Robert Boyars and Robert Orrill (eds), *Laing and Anti-Psychiatry* (Penguin, 1971).

A. Scull, Decarceration: Community Treatment and the Deviant – A Radical View, 2nd edn (Prentice-Hall, 1977) pp. 152–3.

Jeremy Seabrook, *The Idea of Neighbourhood* (Pluto Press, 1984).

Charles D. Shaw, *Introducing Quality Assurance* (King's Fund, 1986).

The Short Report Second Report from the Parliamentary Social Services Committee, 1984–5: *Community Care – with special reference to adult mentally ill and mentally handicapped people*, vol. 1 (HMSO, 1985).

The Skeffington Report; *People and Planning: a Report on Public Participation in Planning* (HMSO, 1960).

Helen Smith (ed.), *Commitment to Quality* (King's Fund, 1989).

Richard Smith, 14 articles on 'Occupationless Health' from 12 October to 14 December 1985 and from 25 January to 15 February 1986, *British Medical Journal*.

P. W. Timms and A. H. Fry, in Dept of Health *Health Trends*, no. 3 vol. 21 (Aug 1989).

Wagner Report, *Residential Care: A Positive Choice* (HMSO, 1988).

Richard Warner, 'Deinstitutionalization: How Did We Get Where We Are?', *Journal of Social Issues*, vol. 45, no. 3 (1989).

Liz Winn and Allison Quick, *User Friendly Services – Guidelines for Managers of Community Health Services* (King's Fund, 1989).

Wolf Wolfensberger, *The Principle of Normalisation* (National Institute of Mental Retardation (Canada), 1972).

Wolf Wolfensberger, *The Origin and Nature of our Institutional Models* (Human Policy Press, 1975).

Women in MIND, *Finding Our Own Solutions – Women's Experience of Mental Health Care* (1986).

World Health Organisation (WHO), *Consumer Involvement in Mental Health and Rehabilitation Services* (Division of Mental Health, 1989).

World Health Organisation (WHO), *Primary Health Care*, Report of the International Conference on Primary Health Care, Alma-Ata, USSR (1978).

4

Match or Mismatch?

Are we producing services aimed at meeting the needs of psychiatric service users or not? Match or mismatch? Broadly, the users have a number of common elements. Although public attitudes are improving, users are still heavily stigmatised and devalued by the rest of the community. They are mostly women and disproportionately black. They are poor, living off social security benefits. They have few friends and social supports. Many still live in the large dormitories of Victorian hospitals or often in poor-quality accommodation in the worst neighbourhoods. Most are anxious and/or depressed. An increasing number are pensioners in rest and nursing homes. Some are homeless, lost on discharge from mental hospitals, living on the wintry streets, begging from passers-by and continually moved on by the police (Brandon *et al.*, 1980). Apart from a select few visionary projects, they have little real influence in the running of their services.

Our psychiatric services are still organised along traditional lines. The move towards 'community care' has been pedestrian. Most long-stay beds are still in the Victorian mental hospitals. There are slowly increasing numbers of community-based day centres, day hospitals, District General Hospital psychiatric units, hostels and group homes.

Progress with the build-up of community-based services has generally been slow, and in some places is not keeping pace with the run-down of long-stay institutions in the NHS. Progress has been slowest for mentally ill people: there are over 25,000 fewer hospital beds than there were ten years ago, but community facilities have not kept pace with only an additional 9000 day care places for example; and no one knows what happens to many people after they are discharged. (HMSO, 1986)

55

Between 1979/80 and 1986/7 the number of local authority
psychiatric day centre places increased by only one thousand to
5,900 and the numbers in all residential homes increased by 3,300
places to a total of 9,200 (HMSO, 1989). In the main, de-
hospitalisation has not meant de-institutionalisation. These newly
developed services are still congregated, professionally dominated
and largely stigmatised – large and small institutions. Even new
services are forms of 'wards in the community', such as the Elderly
Mentally Severely Ill (ESMI) units, the day hospitals and hostels.
They mean improvements in creature comforts; quality of food;
staffing ratios; pleasanter surroundings. All these are important
but involve no real transfer of power from senior management to
junior staff and users, always difficult in huge bureaucracies.

The seemingly good news is that greater numbers of distressed
people are treated outside the formal psychiatric services. Goldberg
and Huxley estimated that out of every thousand people in the
population, roughly 250 have some psychiatric symptoms of whom
230 see their general practitioner. Only 17 become formal psychiatric patients, using out-patient clinics and day hospitals and only 6
from the original thousand become hospital in-patients (Goldberg
and Huxley, 1980).

Most people with 'minor mental illnesses' receive treatment from
their general practitioners, depending on factors like the severity of
the symptoms and the extent of support from family and friends.
However, that treatment consists mainly of various kinds of drugs,
usually tranquillisers and anti-depressants, with major problems of
dependency. Ramon comments: 'The drugging of the majority of
those who express unhappiness can be seen as a major exercise of
social containment of dissatisfaction. But let us not forget that it
also represents a major deviation from the stated value preferences
of every one of the involved professional group' (Ramon, 1985).
Every mental health profession is dedicated to helping people
express and move through despair and anxiety into a more fulfilled
life, mainly through talking, friendship and affection, worthwhile
work and leisure activities. Our ordinary professional practice
takes us far away from those ideals.

The bad news is that 'mental illness' has expanded enormously,
particularly in the latter half of this century. That means an
expansion from the narrow term of 'madness' to more elastic
terms like 'psychological distress' and 'emotional disorder'. These

catch most people most of the time! Human unhappiness has become a technological and individualised problem tackled by technocrats who manipulate complex chemicals sold by huge pharmaceutical companies. At a stroke, human unhappiness is rendered not only unnecessary but almost immoral, because it bothers and disturbs other people. Perhaps there is even a case for forcing people to be less unhappy, less troublesome, to be cheerful (or is it manic?), so they can discover the true meaning of liberty.

Does that sound farfetched? Take this quote in evidence:

> The mass of men lead lives of quiet desperation . . . As Thoreau recognised, depression is part of the human condition. It is consequently the most common of psychiatric illnesses and, given the possibility of suicide, a life-threatening illness at that. Treatment is extremely effective but we often fail to insist on it out of well-intentioned respect for the patient's liberties. If you talk to any depressive after treatment they will tell you that the liberty to experience month after month of black despair is not something we should grant to anyone. (Collee, 1990)

Notice how Thoreau's enlightened quote on the nature and condition of human 'desperation' is shifted into a medical syndrome called 'depression' as well as the use of the devaluing noun 'depressive'.

Dr Collee might have prescribed anti-depressants for the late playwright Samuel Beckett who said: 'I have never had a single untroubled moment in my entire life.' Lennon wrote of him:

> If Beckett was a tormented man it never led you to regard him as an invalid or to treat him like one of the confused, neurotic creatures of which Montparnasse had plenty. What you sensed in him was an inability, or more likely a refusal to turn from an unblinking confrontation with life. So that they may function in some sort of comfort most adults set up in their minds series of screens and distractions to dim the intolerable consciousness of reality which confronts us all – the painful maze that is human relations; inexorable, humiliating decay, and, the insult that renders the whole point of life meaningless – death. Not only in work but in his daily life Beckett refused protective screens. He seemed to stand and stare it out. (Lennon, 1990)

Should chemical treatment have been forced on him and, if so, how many profoundly disturbing plays would have been left us?

Zola comments:

> Basically my contention is that the increasing use of illness as a lever in the understanding of social problems represents no dramatic shift from a moral view to a neutral one but merely to an alternative strategy. Thus, the shift in the handling of such social problems is primarily in those who will undertake the change (psychiatry and other medical specialities) and where the change will take place (in the individual's psyche and body). The problem being scrutinized and the person being changed is no less immoral for all the medical rhetoric. It or he is still a 'problem', though the rhetoric may convince us that he and not the society is responsible, and he and not the society should be changed. Even the moral imperatives remain, in the idea that if such a problem-person can be medically-treated–changed, it–he *should* be. (Zola in Illich *et al.*, 1977)

But how much do we really know about present and potential customers and their perceptions of the services? Surprisingly, not much; but there are fragments. A recent British Medical Journal review notes that 'In the age of the consumer the customer's view is all important. Psychiatric patients are perhaps the last people to be consulted about these matters. This is reflected in the dearth of research on the topic in Britain, though it has drawn attention in the United States' (McIntyre *et al.*, 1989).

The most comprehensive study of patients' perceptions of mental hospitals (King's Fund, 1977) looked at experiences in nine psychiatric hospitals and comments were grouped into four subject areas: the ward, care, hospital life and treatment. Most patients seemed satisfied with their dormitories and day rooms, but had many complaints about the lack of privacy, poor storage facilities and, most of all, noise. Sanitation was criticised less stringently than in general hospitals. The lovely hospital gardens and grounds were much appreciated.

Comments about care indicated that most patients depended heavily on their doctor and felt the need to see him or her at regular intervals. Doctors were greatly appreciated and described as 'sympathetic', 'courteous', 'pleasant' and 'marvellous.' Questions about nurses produced similar enthusiasm. Many patients wanted to know more about their illness from the staff. Comments on hospital life indicated a general trend for long-stay patients to be less critical than short-stay patients.

Views on meals varied considerably, ranging from 'stodgy and inedible' to 'excellent'. Patients were generally appreciative of the occupation/work element in the hospital routine, but over a third complained of having 'nothing to do' at certain times. Blackspots for boredom were evenings and Sundays.

Remarkably, it had been decided that treatment be excluded from the main survey, but many patients volunteered comments. These were usually optimistic, but some were not: 'taking those damned tablets'; 'too much of the needle, nasty side effects'; 'medication very strong'; 'should move forward from drugs'. A few patients were critical of ECT and group therapy. Others remarked on the lack of treatment for physical illnesses within the hospital. Many patients appreciated the mental hospital because it gave asylum – a 'place of retreat and security.

Lonsdale surveyed 100 discharged psychiatric patients living in Hertfordshire:

A very large number of these spent their weekdays at home. Over half the patients were satisfied with the way they spent their time. The majority of those who were dissatisfied tended to be younger, less educated and of a lower socio-economic status. It is apparent that the older patients tend to feel more isolated while it is the young ones who are more dissatisfied with the way they spend their leisure time. The latter group complained of the lack of money to go out in the evenings and weekends – which again may be a problem which they share with their contemporaries who have suffered no psychiatric illness. It may, however, indicate the effects of long-term unemployment and their lack of opportunity to earn the money to meet their needs. (Lonsdale, 1980)

The Birmingham Special Action Project (Ritchie, Morrissey and Ward, 1988) interviewed 67 people with mental illness living in the community. It concluded that 'Not only do they have symptoms of their illness to contend with but their lives are characterised by a lack of paid employment, low income, often fractured/broken relationships and sometimes unsettled living arrangements. Given the complex nature of their problems, it is not surprising to find that people with mental illness feel vulnerable, have little self confidence and low esteem.'

Day centres, despite criticisms, were vitally important for meeting the physical and social needs of some individuals. Others would like paid work. Existing services were seen as far from adequate. The study identified thirteen types of help, which included, advocacy, befriending, carer support; information; companionship; legal, housing and welfare rights advice; emotional support; practical help. In summary their key needs were: to restore confidence and self esteem; to engage in valued activities; personal contact and support; help and support at critical times; occasional sanctuary.

Other surveys covered the London Borough of Hackney and rural Lincolnshire. The Hackney study found that one third of fifty-six long-term patients living in the community felt isolated – 'lack of friends'. Half never took a holiday and another half seldom went out of an evening (Ross, 1981). The Lincolnshire study of hospital in-patients discovered that the existing facilities did little to promote self-worth. There was a shortage of money to provide more homely facilities; and 97 per cent of patients in the hospital rehabilitation unit would prefer a community based placement (Pearce and Halstead, 1985).

Another study was based on interviews with patients at Friern Barnet mental hospital moving into the community (Davis and Towell, 1983). Most patients found the initial announcement of the proposed move a shock. 'In hospitals where the announcement was followed by changes in the ward routine to allow opportunities for the exchange of feelings and worries (e.g. over coffee mornings) patients found support.' It seems that 'staff often feel that they should shield patients for as long as possible from the delays or uncertainties which inevitably occur in the transitional process. This view is not shared by patients who feel less worried by being involved in the ups and downs of negotiation for property and places than being subject to last-minute announcement of changes.'

Patients valued the 'opportunity to create and maintain links with a particular area or possible living situation (e.g. through contact with volunteers from that area) even if the specific details of the move were still uncertain.' Selection for resettlement programmes had to be 'sensitive to the friendships which have grown between people so that the process of personal change does not sweep away personal contacts'.

Many patients experienced 'a gulf between individual learning programmes in the hospital and the demands they were faced with when they left'. Patients valued the space and the time to

> get to know other patients in unsupervised settings before moving out with them. They experienced rehabilitation not so much as teaching new skills but as allowing them the opportunities to display skills which had become rusty since admission and they found programmes which were created for the detailed practical reality of the situations they were moving to much more useful than general preparation for the supposed norms of family or group living.

It is planned to close Friern Barnet hospital in 1991.

Goldie looked at what happened to fifty psychiatric patients discharged from Claybury Hospital (Goldie, 1988):

> One of the striking findings of this study was how few people expressed a desire to be in hospital. Whatever their circumstances, people expressed a preference to retain autonomy and control over their lives, they had gained since leaving hospital . . . One of the inescapable facts is that of the continuing stigmatisation of people as being mental patients . . . the reality of this stigmatisation was such as to effectively restrict people to associating only with others similarly labelled.

Goldie comments that real success was that most lived in normal housing in ordinary neighbourhoods. 'Indeed the greatest contribution to the normalisation of such people would be to significantly increase their incomes, so that they can share with "normal" people such activities as going to the cinema, a public house, or the occasional purchase of new clothes.'

In view of the current debate about keeping open and even expanding long-stay mental hospitals, these former users, however difficult their circumstances, had no wish to return. They valued increased freedom and control over their own lives, found in ordinary localities. Their message was about improving supports and quality of life where they were rather than revamping Victorian institutions.

A study by Leff of 278 long-stay patients discharged from Friern Barnet and Claybury hospitals gives grounds for more optimism. 'These results are more optimistic than the predictions. They show that if you proceed carefully and provide good quality, purpose-built facilities for long-stay patients there are no major disbenefits. Community provision is also slightly cheaper than care in hospital' (*The Independent*, 6 July 1990).

In 1986, after several discussions with senior nursing staff and others, a two day workshop was run in the in-service staff training facility at Prestwich Psychiatric Hospital, Salford. Thirteen residents from Egerton and Heysham, both long-stay male wards, took part in the workshop. Most men were near retirement age or over. Most had been in hospital for more than twenty years. They had few living relatives with whom they had had recent contact and very few outside friendships. These men had limited possessions and little money. They lived, for the most part, in large unattractive dormitories offering little privacy. For all residents, this was the first time in such a workshop and it was also fresh for the nursing staff.

The workshop was designed to uncover the extent of participation, especially by patients, in both the running of the ward and of the hospital. A few patients said a lot. Sometimes their silence had to be encouraged so that more reticent members could say something. Others needed prompting and then spoke out. Some found it easier to make a quiet point during the coffee break out of the earshot of staff. One or two people were difficult to understand so that staff and other residents had to act as interpreters. A few said nothing even when regularly prompted.

A similar workshop was run for both staff and twelve residents from a Lancashire social services department hostel. This was a rehabilitation facility preparing people to return to the community and was run by social service staff with a mixed social work and nursing background. The different workshops showed few real differences between the projects in participation. One overwhelming impression was of the relative powerlessness of both staff and residents. Any analysis of decision-making exposes a considerable centralisation of power and a failure to see these residents as full citizens.

Information systems were woefully inadequate. Both staff and residents often seemed ill-informed of the authorities' policies. They claimed to learn most about Prestwich hospital from local newspapers. At the time, none of the residents knew of the planned rundown and closure of the hospital. Soon after the workshop every patient received a letter giving news of the planned hospital closure. In the hostel, there were no written rules, and this led to confusion about visiting times and other systems.

Some attempts to consult residents had begun. Hospital residents were consulted in drawing up individual care plans. The hostel residents were members of a loosely convened group which planned holidays. In both settings, the purposes of a number of meetings seemed obscure – a complex mixture of politics and therapy. This heady and confusing mixture is a major problem in mental illness services (A. and D. Brandon, 1986).

Studies which ask long-stay patients their views on leaving are rare as frogs in the Sahara desert. Abrahamson tried to interview 309 patients in Goodmayes psychiatric hospital. Some died or were discharged before the interview; others refused; more could not be understood – and so eventually 152 interviews took place (56 per cent) of which 11 per cent were incomplete, mainly through fatigue (Abrahamson *et al.*, 1989). Of those interviewed, 86 per cent did not want to stay permanently in hospital. Paradoxically, 68 per cent responded that they did not want to leave if offered somewhere suitable. Patients seemed well aware of the climate of opinion about closing mental hospitals. Many were interested in leaving but had mixed feelings. They balanced the freedom/independence expected outside in the community with the security and material benefits of living in a large institution. They needed extensive preparation and a realistic experience of various alternatives.

A Manchester University team studied users of mental illness services in Bolton. There were 120 users: hospital in-patients, discharged patients, users of residential facilities, day centres and patients at a depot clinic. One in four expressed serious dissatisfaction with their present accommodation. Only ten had any paid occupation, either full or part-time. Of those without employment, one in four expressed serious dissatisfaction with unemployment. Almost half who lived alone (more than half of the sample) expressed discontent. Some lives were characterised by loneliness and desperation: 70 per cent either had no friends at all or could only identify professionals or other service users as friends. Despite this, the majority were satisfied with their social relationships – low expectations. Only one in three could identify social work help, either at the time of interview or in the previous year. Only one in five could identify help given by a community psychiatric nurse. When help was identified, it was overwhelmingly rated positively (Hatfield, 1990).

'Wounded Healers' provides fascinating evidence about mental health workers' experiences of a 'breakdown' (Rippere and Williams, 1985). It includes material from nineteen contributors who had depression, including psychiatrists, nurses and social workers. After their breakdown they met three kinds of reactions at work from mental health colleagues: active support (accepting them, assuring them that their job was safe: 'You're O.K. We still want to know you'); apparent indifference (not noticing their distress or depression, making no comment); overt hostility (employers trying to get rid of them, hostile reception from colleagues).

In recovery, most wounded healers felt their skills and empathy had improved. A social worker wrote: 'Looking back on my period of depression, I feel it was a turning point in my life. It threw me back on my own resources, and although this was enormously painful at the time, it was the beginning of a long process during which I began to discover what I wanted for myself as an individual rather than as a wife' (Rippere and Williams, 1985, p. 93).

The study concluded that:

> informal contact with mental illness staff/patients could be 'supportive and encouraging'. Incidental displays of human interest, warmth and humour on the part of staff, were appreciated whenever they occurred. But the behaviour of staff, whether medical or nursing, could be extremely unhelpful. Brusqueness, rudeness, a lack of respect/consideration on the part of staff, failure of staff to introduce themselves, or failure to specify when the next appointment would take place were all experienced as unhelpful, as was the constant turnover of staff on one ward. (ibid, p. 181)

How do those various needs, mainly ordinary human ones for dignity, respect, privacy and creature comfort compare with what professionals and services offer? As the potential numbers of customers has expanded, so has the training and both the numbers and variety of professionals involved. We have a growing mental illness industry of counsellors, psychotherapists, psychiatric nurses, social workers, psychologists, psychiatrists – for whom the key element is a therapeutic approach, frequently based on counselling and psychotherapeutic skills. In each locality, there is a large team of professional people with an increasing emphasis on multi-disciplinary work.

But what kind of team is it? Teams can be a minefield of fractured relationships. Professor Sidney Brandon did a study of twenty-three community psychiatric nurses in the Leicester area to assess the care of those with chronic mental illness. They were sceptical of the views of other members of the psychiatric team, particularly the consultant psychiatrists who were 'virtually useless'. They saw social workers as totally redundant, and although slightly more sympathetic to GPs were only happy to give them advice. They saw their main role in giving psychotherapy, especially to those patients with obsessional, compulsive disorders. They rejected functions like monitoring patients' medication and ensuring compliance with medical instructions (Sydney Brandon, 1989). Not much reciprocal respect or effective teamwork there!

Ramon shows how a group of social workers, working in a large mental hospital on a closure programme, became marginalised. Their skills were devalued by the hospital managers and the consultant psychiatrists who saw other professional colleagues, particularly nurses, as doing the 'social work'. They also felt marginalised by their own social services department. Mental illness has a low priority and the local authority was struggling to survive extensive ratecapping (Ramon, 1990).

We have little research comparing user needs with professional skills and attitudes. Foudraine, a Dutch psychiatrist, outlines some of the barriers and resistances towards running more user-sensitive services (Foudraine, 1974). 'Staff need patients quite as much as the patients need staff, if only because their jobs depend on it . . . Staff may need patients to be and to continue to be patients for their own personal reasons. To avoid confronting your own crazy parts by locating them in other people . . . Identification with the system: become part of it by adopting its views and this applies particularly to Doctors.'

The need of staff for jobs, often in areas of high unemployment, is an important element in the resistances to both de-hospitalisation and radical change. Some towns and cities like Lancaster, St Albans and Epsom, surrounded by clusters of long-stay hospitals, with thousands of patients, have more than 10 per cent of their working populations in the mental illness and mental handicap industries. It isn't just individuals and families that rely on work in hospitals and day centres but the whole economies of several towns and many villages. The rundown and closure of large hospitals would have a significant effect on local prosperity.

The situation at Leros, the Greek island with the horrifying facilities for psychiatric and mental handicapped patients, echoed across the world in 1989. The whole issue is much more complex than simply improving facilities for more than a thousand patients living in excrement with not enough to eat. They are a major cash crop for the island. Many local people have no alternative employment other than that of asylum keepers (*The Observer*, 1989). Greek mental illness professionals, despite much higher salaries at Leros, are reluctant to fill the many vacancies.

MacKnight describes a peculiar economic crisis:

Our deficiencies and unmet needs are the ore and coal of the service industries. Thus, the servers called teachers need students. But as their raw material declines, as the baby boom drops off, what do they do? How can they justify their work in the same numbers as the child population decreases? One answer is to 'discover' new needs, unperceived needs, unmet needs – or the need for 'life-long learning'.

 . . . The service economy presents a dilemma: that is the need for need. A million people [in the USA] each year move from goods to service production, the service industry requires more raw material – more need. We can now see that 'need' requires us to discover more human deficiencies . . . We are in a struggle against clienthood, against merely servicing the poor. We must reallocate the power, authority and legitimacy that have been stolen by the institutions of our society. We must oppose those interests of corporate, professional and managerial America that thrive on the dependency of the American people. We must commit ourselves to reallocation of power to the people we serve so that we no longer will need to serve. Only then will we have a chance to realize the American dream: the right to be a citizen and to create, invent, produce and care. (MacKnight, 1980).

Sacks quotes a deaf man during the student strike at the University of Gallaudet, the only university in the world exclusively for deaf students. They were protesting against the appointment of a hearing President. 'This is the first time deaf people ever realized that a colonial client-industry like this can't exist without the client. It's a billion-dollar industry for hearing people. If deaf people don't participate, the industry is gone' (Sacks, 1989). They were breaking through the myth of powerlessness.

For our economic purposes, we need more people like those long-stay psychiatric patients so we can employ more staff. They are our seedcorn. They are worth more distressed and institutionalised than functioning reasonably well. This industry employs hundreds of thousands of people who are trained specifically and expensively (like me) to run mental illness services and to 'help' people with a variety of alleged syndromes. We have a vested interest in seeing the business expand. Those previously described as 'melancholic' are now termed 'clinically depressed' and so become a product. Recently stress syndromes have become fashionable in the posh women's weeklies and monthlies. Almost every month, we invent new mental illnesses with new kinds of so-called experts.

McCord sketches the history of paupers – those not considered directly economically useful:

In general, agencies operate within a social, political, and economic framework that rewards practices which increase the dependency of deviant people on the human service sector . . . Human services enact their role as agents of control by addressing themselves to four overriding tasks: (a) pinpointing the deviant characteristics of people through labelling procedures, and thus assuring society that containment is warranted; (b) keeping deviant people isolated so that society experiences neither the embarrassment nor the burden of caring for such persons; (c) keeping deviant people under control so that society can continue to socialize new members to the accepted boundaries of traditional values and norms; (d) perpetuating deviance by teaching people to conform to their deviant status and to willingly accept their own containment. (McCord, 1982)

Services encourage increased dependency on services. Instead of cash for those in poverty and disability, we give money to secular 'missionaries' like social workers and nurses to 'do good'. Instead of providing reasonable and decent accommodation fostering privacy and dignity, we provide hostels and hospitals, with little user control and autonomy. Marginalisation is accomplished through negatively labelling people and apartheid services where users are herded together. Apartheid means that ordinary people are not troubled by those with mental illness. In these separate and devalued services, people can be controlled/cared for through various therapies including drugs and ECT. People are trained to become 'psychiatric patients', to have low expectations of life; to learn to live on little money; to mix with other distressed people; to be passive; and recognise that they are inferior to the staff.

What does that mean for the practice and training of professionals? Major dangers lie in arrogance and reductionism. Pilgrim is acidic about the contemporary education and skills training of psychologists:

Unfortunately psychology itself has an impersonal tradition which leaves clinical psychologists at the outset of their careers hamstrung by the false hope and security of scientific competence to add to their frequent personal insecurity, which is an intelligible function of relative youth. Technique-oriented workshop manuals peddled by behavioural psychology and psychometric devices are a great comfort to neophyte psychologists but of dubious value to the inevitably complex personal and contextual variation of psychological distress in the real world. (Pilgrim, 1983, p. 1)

Reductionism takes us further away from the customers so avoiding their real pain and distress:

Until sickness came to be perceived as an organic or behavioural abnormality the patient could hope to find in the eyes of his doctor a reflection of his own anguish. What he now meets is the gaze of an accountant engaged in an input/output calculation. His sickness is taken from him and turned into the raw material for an institutional enterprise. His condition is interpreted according to a set of abstract rules in a language he cannot understand . . . Language is taken over by the doctors: the sick person is deprived of meaningful words for his anguish, which is further increased by linguistic mystification. (Illich, 1974, p. 119)

The counselling gimmicks give an illusion of control and achievement. Therapy tricks are used to escape from the pain and poverty of the lives of others who are seen as complex pieces of machinery:

For most people, most of the time, the human way of life ensures self-maintenance; but for a minority, either because of defects of birth, deprivation during childhood, the onset of sickness and old age, the experience of an accident, the shock of bereavement or job loss, or the ill-effects of political, economic or social planning or discrimination, self-sufficiency runs out, and the need for a maintenance mechanic becomes apparent. This need pinpoints the heart of the social worker's role. (Davies, 1985)

Contrast that social mechanic with this position:

The more my practice has developed, the more simple my message has become. Let us start with ourselves, let us not expect our clients to work and heal if we have not done that. Healing is a process and our own process can with awareness and support be a central tool in helping others into and through a process of their own. (Keshet-Orr, 1990)

These two extracts contrast the hearts versus spanners approaches – low-tech or even no-tech versus high-tech. Davies is a macho social work fixer with the modern equivalents of gum and string, working underneath the humanmachine, re-tuning engines and replacing gaskets – a psychology of crypton tuning. Customers engage with a role, a part of the person who is the 'maintenance mechanic'. His power comes from a sense of knowledge and skills, somehow not available to the customer. Keshet-Orr is advocating the giving of the self, not just a role with a spanner but the whole person. She is in the long tradition of the Shamans – the wounded healers.

Rough Times, the radical mental illness magazine of the 1970s, was always pessimistic about spanner shedding:

> By definition, professionalising a skill or area of knowledge means putting a price on it, thereby making it a commodity. To remain in business, a profession must control the production and distribution of its alleged skill, preventing people outside the profession from fully understanding or challenging the profession's authority to be in a business . . . By design, therapists are professionally trained to avoid being human with their patients. Professional standards dictate that the therapist maintains objective, unemotional distance; avoid identifying with the patient's problem; and, most importantly, never give up control of the therapy situation. (*Age*, 1973)

Whatever the nature of interaction, the essential belief is that professionals must call the shots.

The technical language, the professional jargon is an integral part of both the professional tricks, the reductionism and the control. By giving ordinary processes, strange and powerful sounding names, we attain control and mystify:

> Language is not neutral. Feminists like Dale Spender have argued that it is man made and a field of conflict. People with physical disabilities know it is used to handicap and oppress. Words like the 'the old', 'the unemployed', 'the mentally ill' are imposed on us. When we want to be treated on our own terms; for example, as having learning difficulties rather than being 'mentally handicapped', we can expect strong resistance. Language is inseparable from power. (Beresford and Croft, 1988)

Our experiences are taken away and processed by the professional and then returned minus the grit, the smells and discomfort.

Unconsciously, most services discourage staff from emotional involvement with patients. Menzies Lyth, a psychoanalyst, writes about nurses coping with patients' feelings and the trauma of breaking those relationships. 'It is easier for them to deny the feelings and that is what hospitals still encourage nurses to do.' She notes that the hospital dealt with these problems by moving nurses about. She observed that nurses performed lists of tasks almost ritualistically. Precise instructions were given and decisions discouraged so they were relieved of almost all responsibility. Actions were checked and rechecked; decisions were referred upwards, 'leaving staff and students with a very low level of tasks in relation to their ability'. This did little for their self- esteem, personal growth or job satisfaction. They were denied the very things they wanted and expected from nursing – responsibility and close relationships (Menzies Lyth, 1988).

A further study by Forrest on the nature of caring supports this. Nurses got their main source of emotional support from fellow staff nurses. 'Only a nurse with whom one works can understand the emotional burden that arises as a result of caring for acutely ill patients and anxious families' (Forrest, 1989).

A psychiatric nurse writes:

We are all human beings living in a world occupied by other human beings and yet almost every human interaction of the health care professionals denies the undeniable. How often are nurses told they must maintain a professional distance from their patient? The nursing profession moves inexorably towards reductionism. Our need for recognition as a profession has led to an attempt to quantify qualitative action. How can we measure warmth, humour, honesty, wisdom, and respect for fellow human beings? (Jones, 1990)

Here is a description of fine work in a coronary unit:

The conflict between professional distance and emotional involvement has been identified as a central problem for nurses in their care of dying patients. While some nurses may attempt to maintain their professional distance, individualised methods of patient care encourage the development of emotional involvement between nurses and their patients. Where such nursing methods are used it is essential that appropriate ways exist of handling problems which such involvement may cause nurses. In the coronary care unit studied, the organisation of nursing work facilitated close and continuing contact between nurses and their

patients, thereby increasing the chance that emotional involvement would develop. The death of a patient was not viewed by
the nurses as 'failure'; but there were sometimes difficulties for
them arising from their involvement with the patient. (Field,
1989)

One reason for some nurses enjoying their work in the unit was
that it allowed them greater involvement with patients than was
possible in other settings . . . As one registered nurse said: 'It's
only short-term involvement. It's not like your mum or dad or
somebody that you're going to remember the rest of your life. I've
probably got emotionally involved with patients whose names I
couldn't tell you now. But while they were alive and I was looking
after them I was emotionally involved with them. But now it
doesn't bother me.'

Despite the costs, emotional involvement by nurses with dying
patients was more likely to be positive than negative for both nurse
and patient. A system of individualised patient care seems
associated with good nursing care of the dying and also inevitably
creates a certain amount of involvement. 'It is, however, clear that
high levels of involvement may cause difficulties for nurses, and
that many nurses therefore endeavour to limit or avoid it' (Field,
1989).

Roos writes of the more paternalistic and controlling characteristics of the medical model which permeates the human services.
'The relationships between the "ill" person and the "healer" is
structured so as to foster feelings of helplessness, passivity, and
dependency on the part of the former, while generating inappropriate illusions of omnipotence and omniscience on the "healer's"
part. It has been argued that much of the maladaptive behaviour
noted in the institutionalised persons is a function of the staff's
"therapeutic" interaction' (Roos in Wolfensberger, 1971). This
process is dependent on the infantilisation of service users.

Guggenbuhl-Craig describes the 'power shadow' process, where
professionals operate against the wishes of their users. 'In his own
consciousness and to the world at large, the social worker feels
obliged to regard the desire to help as his prime motivation. But in
the depths of his soul the opposite is simultaneously constellated –
not the desire to help, but lust for power and joy in depotentiating
the "client"' (Guggenbuhl-Craig, 1971, p. 10)

One major problem is that, with the limited exception of medicine, professionals get promotion by moving further away from users and into management. Most people in our hierarchical institutions who make the important decisions about patients/clients are those furthest away from ordinary everyday contact.

One important consequence of the major changes in some areas of Italy was that senior professionals were pulled back into serving the ordinary needs of psychiatric patients. De Nicola comments about changing professional roles in the Italian mental illness system (Ramon, 1989):

Making explicit the needs of very regressed patients forced all operators to respond to basic requirements (eating, dressing, acquiring a place for one's belongings) and to put aside their specific professional role. This process of acquiring new knowledge brought about restructuring and the continual questioning of previous roles in the search for new therapeutic strategies. Direct participation became the tool of work: patients, nurses, doctors, social workers, psychologists alike actively participated in morning reports, daily departmental meetings, chairing and minuting general meetings and various committees, for the purpose of examining problems and devising health plans together.

All this facilitated the sharing of anxiety about death and destructiveness connected with mental illness, enabling people to do what one could on the basis of what was required at a given moment instead of 'somebody doing something according to a preordained role'. The doctor's central role became less important, allowing greater autonomy to those below him in the hierarchy. The worker who had the best relationship became the key therapist.

A World Health Organisation document argues for the training of professionals in user issues:

In planning and evaluation, professionals and consumers should respect each other's expertise and experience, with a more balanced weight being given to the views of each. This implies a move away from the assumption that consumers have little insight into their own capabilities and limitations and a move toward recognition of the contribution that consumers can make. The negative attitudes and low expectations which professionals and the lay public sometimes have of the mentally ill should also change. Low performance expectations for consumers of mental health services are likely to doom them to low levels of performance. (WHO, 1989)

Renshaw outlines some imaginative training in Surrey of both users and staff together. 'The high spot of the third workshop was work by Insight, the Brighton-based users group who made everyone sit up and listen and generated fervent discussion.' Users who attended the workshops had very positive things to say about the experience. 'Most found it extraordinary, although gratifying, to stand up and speak as an equal among a group of professionals and, more importantly, to be heard' (Renshaw, 1990).

References

D. Abrahamson *et al.*, 'Do Long Stay Psychiatric Patients Want to Leave Hospital?', *Health Trends*, no. 3 vol. 21, August 1989.

Jeremy Agel, *Rough Times* (Ballantine Books, 1973).

Peter Beresford and Suzy Croft, 'Language for Service Users' *Social Work Today* (11 August 1988).

Althea and David Brandon, *Consumers as Colleagues* (MIND, 1986).

David Brandon *et al.*, *The Survivors* (Routledge & Kegan Paul, 1980).

Sidney Brandon, 'Call for Revamping of CPN Role', *Nursing Times* (29 March 1989).

John Collee, 'A Doctor Writes', *The Observer* (28 Jan 1990).

Martin Davies, *The Essential Social Worker – A Guide to Positive Practice*, 2nd edn (Community Care, 1985).

A. Davis and D. Towell, *Moving Out from the Large Hospitals: Involving the People (Staff and Patients) Concerned* (King's Fund, 1983).

David Field, 'Emotional Involvement with the Dying in a Coronary Care Unit', *Nursing Times* (29 March 1989) pp. 46–8.

Darle Forrest, 'The Experience of Caring', *Journal of Advanced Nursing*, 14(1989) pp. 815–23.

Jan Foudraine, *Not Made of Wood – A Psychiatrist Discovers His Own Profession* (Macmillan, 1974).

David Goldberg and Peter Huxley, *Mental Illness in the Community* (Tavistock, 1980) p. 11.

Nigel Goldie, *I Hated It There, But I Miss the People* (Health and Social Services Research Unit, Southbank Polytechnic, September 1988).

Adolf Guggenbuhl-Craig, *Power in the Helping Professions* (Spring Publications, 1971).

HMSO, *Caring for People: Community Care in the Next Decade and Beyond*, Cm 849 (November 1989).

HMSO, *Making a Reality of Community Care*, A report by the Audit Commission (December 1986).

Barbara Hatfield, 'Bolton Needs Survey', Part III, *Research Report* no 12 (Spring 1990) (Department of Psychiatry, University of Manchester).

Ivan Illich, *Medical Nemesis – The Expropriation of Health* (Calder & Boyars, 1974).

Ivan Illich *et al.*, *Disabling Professions* (Marion Boyars, 1977, pp. 64–5).

The Independent, 'Mentally Ill Fare Well When Freed' (6 July 1990).

Alun Jones, Clinical Nurse Specialist, 'Who Will Care for the Carers?', *The Guardian* (12 January 1990).

Judi Keshet-Orr, 'Allowing emotional responses to emotional situations', *Social Work Today* (1 February 1990).

King's Fund Centre, *Psychiatric Hospitals Viewed by their Patients* (1977).

Peter Lennon, 'Heroes and Villains', *The Guardian Review* (1 February 1990).

Susan Lonsdale, Jolyon Flowers and Betty Saunders, *Long-term Psychiatric Patients: A Study in Community Care* (Personal Social Services Council, 1980).

William T. McCord, 'From Theory to Reality: Obstacles to the Implementation of the Normalization Principle in Human Services', *Mental Retardation*, vol. 20, No. 6 (1982) p. 248.

John J. McGee *et al.*, *Gentle Teaching – A Non-Aversive Approach to Helping Persons with Mental Retardation* (Human Sciences Press, 1987).

John L. MacKnight, 'Social Services and the Poor: Who Needs Who?', *Public Welfare* (Washington, USA) (Autumn 1980).

K. McIntyre, Michael Farrell and Anthony David, 'What Do Psychiatric Inpatients Really Want?', *British Medical Journal*, vol. 298 (21 January 1989) pp. 159–60.

Isabel Menzies Lyth, *Containing Anxieties in Institutions* (Free Association Books, 1988).

The Observer, 'Europe's Guilty Secret – 1,300 Lost Souls Left to Rot' (10 September 1989).

Jeanne Pearce and Jeremy Halstead, *Lives in the Balance – A Study of the Quality of Residential Services in North Lincolnshire for People with Long Term Psychiatric Problems* (North Lincolnshire Health Authority, 1985).

David Pilgrim (ed.), *Psychology and Psychotherapy – Current Trends and Issues* (Routledge, 1983, p. 1).

Shulamit Ramon, *Psychiatry in Britain – Meaning and Policy* (Croom Helm, 1985, p. 319).

Shulamit Ramon, *Psychiatry in Transition* (Croom Helm, 1989).

Shulamit Ramon, 'Social Work Teams Facing the Closure of a Psychiatric Hospital' (unpublished 1990).

Judy Renshaw, Frances Jones and Cathie Andrews, 'Community Mental Health: Making Headway in Training' (unpublished February 1990).

Vicky Rippere and Ruth Williams (eds), *Wounded Healers – Mental Health Workers Experiences of Depression* (John Wiley, 1985).

Jane Ritchie, Catrin Morrissey and Kit Ward, *Keeping in Touch with the Talking – the Community Care Needs of People with Mental Illness* (S.C.P.T., March 1988).

Gwynneth Ross, 'Survey: Lifestyle of Long-term Psychiatric Patients in the London Borough of Hackney' (Psychiatric Rehabilitaton Association, Dec 1981).

D. L. Rosenhan, 'On Being Sane in Insane Places', *Science*, 179(1973) pp. 250–8.

Oliver Sacks, *Seeing Voices* (Picador, 1989) p. 156.

P. O. Sandman, A. Norberg and R. Adolfsson, 'Verbal Communication and Behaviour During Meals in Five Institutionalized Patients with Alzheimer-type Dementia', *Journal of Advanced Nursing*, 13(1988) pp. 571–8.

Wolf Wolfensberger, *Principle of Normalisation* (National Institute for Mental Retardation, Canada, 1971).

World Health Organisation (WHO), Division of Mental Health, *Consumer Involvement in Mental Health and Rehabilitation Services* (1989).

5

Telling People Much Much More

This chapter examines the inadequate communication about mental illness. Many users complain about insufficient information, often confusing and inaccurate. What are the obstacles to telling people much, much more? Why is relevant and accurate information often not sensitively given? Who else is entitled to know the personal and private details given to mental illness professionals and under what conditions?

Many obstacles are structural. To possess knowledge and keep others in ignorance is immense power, useful to fuel ambition. If societies see mental illness as somehow shameful, making it difficult for people to talk about their depression and despair, communication gets constipated. If people are treated badly, their rights often violated, our social structures are not likely to broadcast such violations.

We have a serious information problem. The seminal study is by Lidz in the USA which showed that psychiatric patients' understanding was 'typically incomplete and occasionally badly misdirected.' 'Perhaps more important, it seemed often to be idiosyncratic and experientially based . . . disclosure by staff, even when fairly substantial, seemed to play a relatively small part in the patients understanding of their problems' (Lidz *et al.*, 1984, p. 317). The study distinguished different elements in information. (ibid, p. 316) It was usually given after rather than before decisions were made. It was not designed to help autonomy but to assist the effectiveness of the treatment plan. Patients were not consulted about the nature of treatment, only about its application.

Information was given by many different people. It was unclear who was responsible for telling the patient what was going on. The researchers called this 'floating responsibility'. Disclosure was often brief and incomplete. In some cases relevant information was not given and in other cases 'staff contradicted each other.' Staff were less likely to provide information to patients considered to have limited intelligence and/or to be less psychologically healthy. Researchers found no evidence to suggest that disclosure had ever caused harm. Significantly, most patients believed that decisions about treatment were for the physician (ibid, p. 318).

'Only rarely do doctors believe that there are two "alternatives", equally good treatments available for a particular condition. Rather there are more desirable treatments and less desirable treatments, and it makes little sense to inform the patients of the alternative treatments, since the patient lacks the skill and experience necessary to make the right choice.' Note the masculine emphasis on getting the 'right choice' and the consequent devaluing of the joint responsibility for decision making.

A good flow of accurate information, sensitively communicated, reduces stress and assists in recovery from illness. Florence Nightingale commented:

> Apprehension, uncertainty, waiting, expectation, fear of surprise, do a patient more harm than any exertion. Remember he is face to face with his enemy all the time, internally wrestling with him, having long imaginary conversations with him . . . Do not forget that patients are shy of asking . . . It is commonly supposed that a nurse is there to save physical exertion. She ought to be there to save the patient taking thought. (Nightingale, 1859)

More than a century later, medical researchers wrote on the same theme:

> There does now seem to be empirical evidence to support the belief that many important outcomes of medical practice are dependent on the interpersonal skills, and particularly the empathic skills of the practitioner . . . Non-psychiatric studies typically assume that the Dr needs two important skills: (a) to be able to provide conditions in a consultation in which the patient can accurately transmit information about his history,

symptoms, worries and so on; (b) to be able to 'decode' non-verbal and verbal signals provided by patients. (Walton, 1986, p. 54)

Increasing information is central to the consumer movement whether in social services or in car manufacture. Ralph Nader, founding father of the American consumer movement, wrote 'the public has never been supplied with the information nor offered the quality of competition to enable it to make effective demands through the market place . . . The task of the consumer movement now is to gather and analyse and disseminate information by demanding it and by mounting private actions by consumer groups to publicise it' (Nader, 1973).

Increasing information needs whistle blowers – troops inside the machine. They know how industries really work, possess privileged secrets and can help reform or destroy from within. 'An individual must have a right to blow the whistle on his organisation . . . rather than be forced to condone illegality . . . oppression of the disadvantaged . . . or the like.' Whistle blowing would generate critical information providing a real 'potential for change when that (external) pressure forges an alliance with people of conscience within the institution' (Chu and Trotter 1974).

Systems see whistle blowers as threatening and try to counter their subversion, although seldom with the zeal of Tower Hamlets Health Authority. Jeff Prosser, unit general manager of community services, wrote to all staff reminding them that it was forbidden to contact MPs, journalists, councillors or health authority members, without prior permission. He added that 'a breach of these instructions could result in disciplinary proceedings' (Laurance, 1988).

Prosser represents a long tradition. Titmuss noted that 'The barrier of silence is one device employed to maintain authority.'

What is it that patients complain of more than anything else in relation to the hospital – 'No one told me anything' – 'Nobody asked me' – 'I don't know'. How often one comes across people who have been discharged from hospital, bewildered, still anxious and afraid; disillusioned because the medical magic has not apparently or not yet yielded results, ignorant of what the investigations have shown, what the doctors think, what the treatment has been or is to be, and what the outlook is in terms of life and health. (Titmuss, 1958, p. 127)

He went even further: 'Criticism from without of professional conduct and standards of work tends to be increasingly resented the more highly these groups are organised' (ibid, p. 27). Historically, such criticism has been bitterly resented, as the side effects of half a dozen scandal enquiries on large mental hospitals in the 1970s illustrated. Beardshaw notes:

Nurses have good reasons for keeping quiet about abuse in mental hospitals: silence is a normal, human response to intimidation and fear. Their silence is enforced by vested interests within the hospital organisation: interests which have something to hide or which prefer not to face embarrassing, painful and difficult truths . . . This enforced silence involves a denial of basic human rights. Through it patients suffer within a 'caring' environment. Through it caring nurses are deprived of free speech and are effectively prevented from following their professions basic tenets. (Beardshaw, 1981, p. 81)

Graham Pink, a charge nurse, spoke out against poor staffing and conditions in psycho-geriatric services in Stockport. His national nursing council supported him. A colleague drawing up a petition to support his case wrote to her Unit Manager: 'I know most of my colleagues agree with him on this matter but, unfortunately, many were reluctant to sign a petition fearing recriminations. It has come to my knowledge that I have already been branded a "troublemaker" for my efforts. Those signatures I already have I now feel reluctant to pass on to you for fear of further recriminations against them' (Brindle, 1990).

Two key issues for individual patients are: how much confidential material is passed on to other professionals and relatives? and what is the quality and quantity of information received from their mental illness professionals. The Hippocratic Oath states: 'Whatever, in connection, with my professional practice, or not in connection with it, I see or hear, in the life of men, which ought not to be spoken of abroad, I will not divulge, as reckoning that all such should be kept secret.' Confidentiality is important in professional practice. All professions lay great importance on restricting the flow of information about patients/clients. They recognise that private and personal information about individuals, particularly their misfortunes and sicknesses, should be restricted. But restricted to whom? Who is to decide and on what grounds?

As we saw in the 'Mismatch' chapter, professional practice mixes care and control. Many professional functions are forms of social policing. Information can be used to enhance the interests of the agencies which pay us – for example, data provided about the apparent fecklessness of families to justify housing evictions but not in the interests of families rendered homeless.

The BMA makes seven major exceptions to strict confidentiality. These are: if a patient consents; if it is in the patient's own interests that information should be disclosed, but it is either impossible or medically undesirable in the patient's own interests to get his consent; if the law requires (and does not merely permit) the doctor to disclose the information; if the doctor has an overriding duty to society to disclose the information; if the doctor agrees that disclosure is necessary to safeguard national security; if the disclosure is necessary to prevent a serious risk to public health; in certain circumstances, for the purposes of individual research' (BMA, 1982). All those exclusions make it difficult for the user to appreciate the real meaning of confidentiality. When he tells the doctor/social-worker/nurse something, who else has the right to know?

The fundamental principle is that the doctor 'must not use or disclose any confidential information which he obtains in the course of his professional work for any purpose other than the clinical care of the patient to whom it relates . . . A patients general authority may be assumed for the necessary sharing of information with other professionals concerned with his health care.' What does a vague phrase like 'clinical care' really mean?

Breaching confidentiality is justified in the 'patients best interests'. The assumption is that he or she is no longer the best judge and that others – professionals and family and friends – are better. Professionals, with considerable vested interests particularly concerning those large organisations paying their salaries, so frequently at odds with their obligations to the patient, make those 'better judgements' (BMA, 1982).

Helen Smith notes:

> confidentiality underpins the status of workers, yet they con-
> tinually breach it, usually without asking the individual, when
> liaising with other disciplines and agencies: users know this
> happens. Confidentiality, presented to them as being necessary
> for their care and the coordination of services, is preserved as
> part of the caring relationships and broken for the same reason.
>   This double-bind situation 'submerges' users; they become
> unable to challenge the breach of confidence if they wish to gain
> access to certain services. If workers are to change their
> relationships with users they must clearly state their rules of
> play. So far as confidentiality is concerned, it must be made clear
> when and what information will be given without the user's
> permission; when (written) permission will be sought; and what
> information will be strictly confidential to a particular worker or
> groups of workers. (Smith, 1989)

The second key issue is withholding information from patients.
Atkinson examines detailed arguments against telling of a diagnosis of schizophrenia: 'Firstly the dictate "do no harm" is
invoked, allowing the doctor to override other issues such as
charges of deception or the individual's rights to truth and
information. Harm is usually taken to mean adding to the
patient's problems by creating or increasing despair, anxiety or
depression, and in psychiatric illness, we may add low self-esteem'
(Atkinson, 1989). The doctor is the sole judge of what is harmful.
Higgs comments wisely: 'No other profession sees it as their duty
to suppress information simply to preserve happiness' (Higgs in
Lockwood, 1985, p. 196).

'A further area of "harm" has to be considered in psychiatry,
and that is the social effect of being labelled 'schizophrenic' – the
negative aspects of official labelling' (Atkinson, 1989). This seems
tautological. We define someone as having a certain condition but
can't tell him because of the harm done by the label! He still suffers
from the damaging psychiatric label whilst being denied the
knowledge of it. This has echoes of Kafka's *The Trial* in which
K cannot find out the accusations made against him.

A related argument is the uncertainty principle. 'The medical
practitioner may be misinformed or the situation indeterminate.

Neat summary may be difficult if not impossible' (Gillett, 1989). No doctor can ever be completely sure of the diagnosis or prognosis, particularly of schizophrenia. But a medical practitioner is constantly dealing with uncertainties and is required to make an honest judgement rather than be absolutely correct, by its nature unreasonable.

Some professionals argue that more information increases confusion. Ingelfinger suggests that 'Increasing detail may often lead to increasing confusion and exaggerated fear for patients' (Ingelfinger, 1972). The BMA deals firmly with this:

> Doctors sometimes argue that patients do not want to be told all the facts. In an increasingly articulate society Doctors are moving away from this paternalistic approach and any Doctor who decides to withhold information should examine stringently the reason for doing so. Society is moving away from paternalism towards partnership and at the same time people are taking increasing responsibility for the effects of their own way of life including its effects on health. (BMA, 1989, p. 29)

When asked, some patients may not want to know their diagnosis. That is not confined to psychiatry and frequently arises in conditions like cancer. On one level this is simple. You ask the patient whether she wants to know and she responds either by saying Yes or No or by being uncertain.

Some practitioners argue that diagnostic revelations may adversely effect the doctor–patient relationship: 'Since people with schizophrenia usually lack insight, to tell them they are schizophrenic will not be accepted and will therefore be pointless; or to give this information to people who are paranoid will only increase their paranoia as they will believe the doctor has now turned against them' (Atkinson, 1989). This is a clear tautology with so many generalisations about schizophrenia that they are difficult to unravel. Some people do have insight whatever that difficult term means, but even if they do not, does withholding information help treatment? Not providing information can contribute to paranoia.

Lack of information makes the concept of informed consent in the 1983 Mental Health Act (Part IV on Consent to Treatment) impossible. What is 'informed' to mean? The relationship between doctor and patient should be a partnership based on the patient's informed consent to the treatment. This has no reality without the patient being in full possession of the facts. Richard Jones' footnotes on the 1983 Act remind us that 'Valid consent implies the ability, given an explanation in simple terms to understand the nature, purpose and effect of the proposed treatment' in an 'atmosphere which is uncontaminated by fear or intimidation' (Jones, 1982).

Herbert provides an even clearer definition: 'that consent which is obtained after the patient has been adequately instructed about the ratio of risk and benefit involved in the procedure as compared to alternative procedures or no treatment at all' (Herbert, 1988). However, 'ratio of risk and benefit' is a very difficult equation in such a hazy field.

Perry notes that 'certain affective disorders are associated with compromised or diminished cognitive and emotional capacities and thus, with one's ability to act as a fully autonomous individual' (Perry, 1985). Given those circumstances, how is 'adequately instructed' to be defined and achieved? Where it is agreed that the patient is incapable of meaningful communication, information is given to relatives/friends. They would be involved in decisions. Where there are no relatives, citizen advocates external to the service delivery systems and with few vested interests can help.

Dworkin examined the situation of someone with dementia:

> consider the rights, not of someone who was born and always has been demented, but of someone who has been competent in the past. We may think of that person, as the putative holder of rights, in two different ways: as a demented person, in which case we emphasise his present situation and capacities, or as a person who has become demented, in which case we emphasize that his dementia has occurred in the course of a larger life whose whole length must be considered in any decision about what rights he has. (Dworkin, 1986)

As a general principle, it is reasonable to assume that a person with dementia can understand more than it seems to us.

Bingley and Lacey outline some technical arguments in favour of preventing or restricting access to casefiles (Bingley and Lacey, 1988). Disclosure of medical records might deter doctors from being frank. There are few reasonable arguments against doctors writing for themselves rough notes which speculate about the patient's condition but this does not justify the secrecy of medical records.

Some argue that medical records are too technical for the layman. This assumes the lack of capacity to understand or to acquire the necessary understanding. Are records unnecessarily complex? How good are our communication skills? Beresford and Croft write:

> the language of files may make them less accessible to service users because they are primarily designed for professionals. But the issue is not just one of jargon which besets all spheres of specialised human activity. Social work language, like that of other human service organisations and professions, can be part of a process of mystification, exclusion and disassociation. It's a short step from talking about someone's 'verbal aggression' to conceiving of the problem as lying within them rather than having wider connections or being related to us. Issues are reduced to personal characteristics. (Beresford and Croft, 1988)

A World Health Organisation paper states that users have a right to freedom from stigmatizing labels:

> Once so labelled, they (service users) can be stigmatized and ostracized for life. Many admit that mental distress can be debilitating but wish to see an alternative approach taken to diagnosis and labelling. This approach would not necessarily deny that biological factors can play a part in causing mental health distress, but would assert that the bulk of mental health problems are related to social, environmental and familial reasons. The proponents of this approach argue that diagnostic labels ascribe the problem to some deficit or personal wrong doing and imply that the person is responsible in some way. Diagnostic labels of mental illness tend to stick with a person for the rest of his life and may have profound negative consequences which follow the individual and often interfere with achievement of routine and normal activities such as applying for jobs, getting a driver's licence, opening a bank account, securing a loan, purchasing property, etc. (WHO, 1989)

Whatever people's rights to information, third parties may need protection. Frequently, information contained in a patient's medical records has been obtained from others, for example, family members, neighbours, employees of other agencies or other professionals. If they had known such information would be disclosed to the patient then they might not have provided it. Such sources can be kept confidential if people have objections to revelation but that should not necessarily include professionals.

Another argument about withholding information arises from the fear of litigation. In giving more information to patients, this argument runs, there is a risk of lighting a forest fire of legal actions. This implies scandals covered by secrecy. If there are injustices, malpractices, the flouting of people's rights, why shouldn't the courts deal with them? Fears of 'vexatious litigation' are based on a belief that patients, particularly those compulsorily detained, have strong tendencies to take unjustified revenge through the law, so professionals, particularly psychiatrists, need protection because the courts cannot discern the differences between justified and unjustified suits. There is little evidence for such a belief.

Both the 1959 Mental Health Act and its successor the 1983 Act placed severe restrictions on access to the courts by patients (Gostin, 1975). Under the 1983 Act the litigant has to demonstrate that a particular act(s) was done in bad faith or without reasonable care. 'No civil proceedings shall be brought against any person in any court in respect of any such act without the leave of the High Court; and no criminal proceedings shall be brought against any person in any court in respect of any such act except by or with the consent of the Director of Public Prosecutions' (section 139). This is another hurdle in the legal steeplechase for mental illness patients.

These arguments for restricting information help clarify some technical problems. With particular safeguards, most difficulties can be overcome. However, the underlying problem of paternalism remains. As professionals we are seeking to protect others allegedly more vulnerable than ourselves, unable to make mature judgements. On one level, those protective tendencies are deeply hidden. On another they are exposed to users. They reflect an assumption that the relationships in which we are involved not only are but should be profoundly unequal; that we are able to look clearly at life and for the most part get full and accurate information about what is happening and that many others, particularly those with severe mental illnesses, are incapable of dealing with such information. That assumption damages both ourselves and the patients.

A sociologist suggests that doctors withhold information to reduce their own stress levels. In her Canadian study of 118 women patients being told for the first time at a health clinic that they had cancer, she examined the behaviour of the doctors:

> Physicians remain unconvinced that it is always in the patient's best interests to give full details of their case . . . At this clinic, the topic of what and how physicians tell their patients was never formally discussed, had not been included in medical training, and was not considered a topic warranting serious research. Clinic physicians adopted a policy of disclosing information based on a [their] personal comfort level . . . Despite continuing personal discomfort, they preferred to develop techniques and policies to reduce that tension rather than confront the issue directly.

They were not able to deal with telling people all the bad news and unable to share those difficulties with colleagues and receive help. Consequently, their patients suffered unnecessarily (Taylor, 1988).

Do people have any right not to know? Intentional or pseudo ignorance has important consequences for professionals. We can become unwilling keepers of dark secrets. If some people refuse to be informed about drug side-effects, for example, what are the consequences for us? 'It's O.K. doctor. I leave all that sort of thing to you.' Is that definition of the relationship between doctor, social worker, nurse, one we can readily accept with its omnipotent implications ? The World Health Organisation Alma-Ata declaration places not only a right on patients but a 'duty to participate individually and collectively in the planning and implementation of their health care' (WHO, 1978).

> Workers are usually expected to present themselves as successful, responsible, caring, emotionally mature and self-confident. It seems to me that this has several damaging effects . . . most of us find it impossible to be this all the time. We desperately push away any doubts, anxieties and sadness we feel during a usually

stressful working day and quietly collapse off duty feeling ourselves to be emotional frauds! . . . it's easier for workers to create this desired self-image if they see service users (and implicitly train them to see themselves) as ill, dependent, childishly manipulative, selfish and lacking in abilities . . . the super-human model of normality that workers embody can be discouraging. (Lowson, 1989)

There is little analysis of the costs of wearing that cloak of power, which I call the Icarus Syndrome after the son of Daedalus, who flew too close to the sun in the Greek legend. The question is not so much whether patients can handle the emotional consequences of relevant information or not, but whether we, as professionals, can handle playing God. There is evidence that we cannot. Our mental illness professions have some of the highest rates of alcoholism, attempted suicide and actual suicide rates. Trying to carry divine responsibilities, with little support, can be a contributing factor to personal distress.

Looney interviewed 263 psychiatrists in the USA. Of these, 73 per cent reported experiences of moderate to incapacitating anxiety during their early practice years, and 58 per cent had experienced serious depression (Looney *et al.*, 1980). Bermak's study of American psychiatrists indicated that 90 per cent expressed a wide variety of different mental illnesses (Bermak, 1977). 'Psychiatrists commit suicide at a rate which is four times to five times greater than that of the general population' (Guy, 1987).

Atkinson details the positive arguments for increased information. There is a moral argument which centres around the patients 'right to know'. Medical records contain information that is private and personal to the patient/client and he has a basic right to that information. Not telling him is the equivalent of lying to patients. Where relatives but not the patient is told, which is common in psychiatric circles, his autonomy is further undermined. Whose health is it anyway? Atkinson and Coia suggest that 'the crucial issue seems to be whether patients have the right to an exclusive relationship with their doctor when the illness/behavioural problem has an impact on all the family, and relatives are involved in providing care for the patient' (Atkinson and Coia, 1990). Such dilemmas should be discussed extensively, particularly with the patient.

We could be more open about breaches of confidentiality. Patients could be told they are receiving incomplete information and given the reasons. Patients could also be told that relatives are being given information against their wishes: 'I asked you several days ago whether I could tell your relatives about your illness because the nocturnal restlessness and general aggressive behaviour has a direct impact on their lives, in living with you. You said No – not on any account. I have given this matter considerable thought and I've decided to inform them anyway. I have responsibilities to them as well. This is what I intend to tell them . . .'

Yet another argument is that withholding the diagnosis inflates its importance. Diagnosis is seen as a solution to human problems and the patient as a passive object of medical conjuring tricks. Informing the patient demystifies the process and makes him an ally and partner. It may help alleviate guilt and assist in treatment and the search for meaning. For example, the patient may be able to detect early warnings of a relapse when the diagnosis has been fully explained (Masnik, 1974). One piece of research in Livingston, near Edinburgh, involved patients in reporting adverse drug reactions (Campbell and Howie, 1988).

In practice, the patient may find out anyway. Radio, TV and magazines are a rich source of knowledge about mental illness. Public sources of information are a serious concern to professionals. Some people are left confused and half-informed, particularly through reports of 'miracle cures'. One hospital-based psychiatrist comments sardonically: 'If nothing else they can read it in the papers, and a lot of what you read in the papers is inaccurate' (Kempson, 1987). Whose fault is that? Is it that journalists are writing inaccurate and sensational articles? Do we give clear information to patients and to journalists writing stories?

If patients find out that information has been concealed, it can seriously disrupt the professional relationship. Openness is a significant component of trust, particularly where people have considerable power. 'Whether or not knowing the truth is essential to the patient's health, telling the truth is essential to the health of the Dr–patient relationship' (Higgs, 1985, p. 202). Telling only the family can increase tensions and relatives are put in an impossible practical position. They may have to lie or give false reassurances, denying their own distress.

Access to files enables the correction of inaccuracies:

Lyle Clarke, a 27 year old man, who is mentally handicapped, was admitted to Rampton Special Hospital in 1972, aged 16, from a local hospital. His medical records indicated that he had sexually assaulted an eight-year-old child and bitten off the head of a chicken. His records also indicated that he was 'aggressive'. Mr Clarke's case was referred to a Mental Health Tribunal in 1983 and it was discovered that many alleged facts in his medical records, including those above, were wrong or grossly exaggerated. Mr Clarke and his family had never been able to see his records and therefore it was only when they were leaked to the press that his relatives were able to ensure that they were put right. (Bingley and Lacey, 1988)

Increased information from health and social service professionals is an important part of the whole movement towards more freedom of information. Some progress has been made in recent years in giving people more rights. The 1986 Disabled Persons (Representation) Act requires a local authority to give to any disabled person, receiving a service, clear information about its services.

Under the Access to Personal Files Act, 1987, anyone outside Northern Ireland, who is the subject of personal information held by social service departments (SSDs) gained new rights. Any individual making a written request for access to personal information must be told by the relevant department whether such information is held. There must be a reply within forty days. If information is not intelligible, the SSD must give an explanation. If the terms are professional or technical and are still not understood, the individual should be able to go to someone else for advice. The Act advises the SSDs to consider interpretative counselling to minimise possibility of harm to anyone from what has been learned.

There are six grounds for restriction or refusal of access, of which the most important is, if: serious harm to the physical or mental health or emotional condition of the individual, or of someone else, would result, which could include a staff member. This is seen as an exceptional circumstance and must apply only to particular pieces of information.

If an individual is unhappy with the decision on access he or she has the right of appeal, within twenty-eight days, to a committee of three of the local authority's elected councillors – only one of whom may be on the social services committee. The appeal may be in writing or orally before the committee. General rights of remedy through the courts or ombudsman are not restricted. Individuals may write asking the SSD to correct 'inaccuracies' in information provided (Dolan, 1989).

The Access to Medical Reports Act 1988 gives access to medical reports relating to the individual, supplied by a medical practitioner for employment or insurance purposes. There seems to be increasing opinion amongst doctors that a far wider access to records would be helpful and acceptable. In a Birmingham study of increased patient participation in general practice where there was assisted access to medical records, 82.4 per cent of patients involved said that it had been helpful (Bird *et al.*, 1988).

The government White Paper *Working for Patients* suggests that hospitals should offer 'clear information leaflets about the facilities available and what patients need to know when they come to hospital. . . . once someone is in hospital, clear and sensitive explanation of what is happening – in practical matters such as where to go and who to see, and/or clinical matters, such as the nature of an illness and its proposed treatment' (Department of Health, 1989, para 1.13).

More specifically, the Code of Practice on the 1983 Mental Health Act states:

All patients should be given, throughout their stay in hospital, as much information as possible about their care and treatment . . . Requests for information from the patient should be encouraged and answered honestly and comprehensively. Periodic checks should be made to ensure that patients continue to understand the information given to them. The purpose of information is to help people understand why they are in hospital. In particular it is important that informal patients understand their right to leave hospital. (Dept of Health, 1990)

There has been an information explosion about mental illness. Bookshops of any size have shelves of relevant material. The MIND factsheets explore in a simple and attractive format a whole range of issues: compulsory detention; schizophrenia; manic depressive psychosis; ECT; depression. Sheldon Press publish a

range of popular books on anxiety, depression, stress. Mental
health and mental illness have become prime topics for magazines,
radio and TV: 'LOWER YOUR PERSONAL STRESS', 'BIG
BREAKTHROUGH IN SCHIZOPHRENIA', 'IS ALCOHOL-
ISM A THREAT TO YOUR RELATIONSHIPS', 'MENTAL
PATIENTS SLEEP OUT ON LONDON STREETS'. For example,
the Esther Rantzen prime time TV programme *That's Life*
campaigned with MIND on anti-depressant drugs and their
dependency problems, during the mid-1980s.

Information for relatives and other carers is also growing.
MIND produces a leaflet called *Understanding Caring* 'to help
you give emotional support to a friend or relative who is
experiencing mental health problems. It also offers advice about
handling difficult situations that may arise and suggests ways of
looking after yourself' (MIND, 1989).

Most statutory services have not been part of that explosion.
NHS and social services typically provide inadequate information
about their services. Probably, this stems from fears, mostly
unjustified, that more general knowledge about their services will
mean being increasingly overwhelmed by demands. The sparse
information provided is often characterised by difficult terms, low-
quality text and poor design.

Some services, including many not-for-profit organisations, are
very imaginative. They have produced original and low-cost videos
so that people can get an action shot of services. These videos or
more traditional sound/slide shows give visitors, newcomers, or
potential users, a vigorous introduction.

One promising but limited development is the establishment of
Citizen Advice Bureaux in some large mental hospitals, some of
which are under financial threat through cutbacks in funding. They
provide accurate information in locations which were often remote
and isolated, but it has not been without resistance. The Gateshead
branch, setting up an extension office, reported in 1981:

> While administrative staff have been extremely helpful towards
> the bureau, liaison and co-operation with other members of staff
> is practically non-existent. Medical staff have proved unhelpful
> and they have made no referrals. A CAB pilot scheme at
> Ronkswood Hospital, Worcester, met with a distinct lack of
> co-operation between administration and hospital workers and a

restrictive paternalistic attitude towards CAB on the part of the staff (Faulkner, 1986).

We found in Prestwich mental hospital where there was a CAB office that many long-stay patients did not know of its function or existence (A. and D. Brandon, 1987) Information services aimed at long-stay populations, in particular, should be more active in going on to the wards with information.

Information given to individuals about their condition has to be sensitively communicated. In a recent study, 41 per cent of patients were dissatisfied with the information given by their GP regarding their mental illness (MIND/Roehampton, 1990). Much needed is information which lays out various options for the person and their likely consequences. We need to communicate in ways that can be easily understood and recalled. Patients prefer written information which can be read and re-read in private and discussed with others (*The Lancet*, 1989). Research shows that we tend to forget half of what the doctor tells us. Especially worrying is that we have difficulty remembering the most crucial advice of all – about treatment. Older patients, especially those taking lots of drugs, are particularly vulnerable. When forty-six cancer patients were given cassette tapes of their 'bad news' consultations to take home, both patients and families 'benefited enormously' from the chance to hear details of their diagnosis and treatment again. Many patients felt that the primary value of the tape was its usefulness in giving accurate information to families (Illman, 1990).

Lambeth MIND holds discussions with users on long-stay wards about moving them into the community. They have developed a simple game which prompts discussion on various aspects of housing, and have assembled a set of slides and a large set of cards for use in hospital, to provide information to users and encourage thinking about the future (Lambeth MIND, 1988). The Residents' Rights Project has just produced an impressive and sophisticated handbook and accompanying interactive video to help people with learning difficulties understand their housing rights in the community (Allen and Scales, 1990).

O'Brien developed a 'Getting to Know You' exercise which is based on at least 24 hours observation of a person with disabilities. This allows a person to 'get a feel' of the patient's day. The exercise has to be a single minded task and preferably done by someone who is an outsider with few preconceived ideas (Brost and Johnson, 1982).

We need to be more skilled in providing information to people. A social worker showed a casefile to a client where accusations had been made by neighbours that she was starving and ill-treating her two-year-old. The client appreciated the access to her file. The social worker concludes:

> There are obvious gains in honesty and openness. Greater clarity is needed about the status of information, and it can sometimes feel as if a course in linguistics is needed to appreciate fine distinctions about fact and inference which are all too easily blurred . . . Official activities enmeshed in mystique and secrecy cause untold damage, both to individuals and to the structure of the society we live in. Surely it is the secrecy that is harmful.
> (Cornwell, 1990)

In some situations, showing files to clients can grow towards some sort of joint responsibility for writing a true record (Neville and Beak, 1990).

More information should be and increasingly is being provided in a wider range of formats like braille and various languages, particularly those of ethnic minorities. Some people whose reading abilities are impaired, including those with learning difficulties, are probably best served by case records on audiotape.

A United States Presidents Commission suggested a number of principles about communicating information (Presidents Commission, 1982). 'Seeing that professionals possessed certain interpersonal skills and attitudes; willingness of patients to participate; non jargon language; written and audio visual materials; proper time/ space with financial implications for professionals accepted; pamphlets on medications; opening up medical libraries to the public.

Beardshaw comments more succinctly:

> Managing disability well involves developing good coping strategies. This requires professional and client to exchange information freely and agree goals to create the best possible strategy for dealing with problems. There is ample evidence to

suggest that this kind of exchange is the exception rather than the rule. In practice prescriptive methods still appear to dominate professional practice, despite lip service towards partnership. (Beardshaw, 1988)

References

Peter Allen and Kate Scales, *Residents' Rights – Helping People with Learning Difficulties Understand Their Housing Rights* (Residents Rights Project, 1990).

Jacqueline M Atkinson, 'To Tell or Not to Tell the Diagnosis of Schizophrenia', *Journal of Medical Ethics* (1989) pp. 21–4.

J. M. Atkinson and D. A. Coia, 'Responsibility to Carers – An ethical dilemma', *Psychiatric Bulletin* (1990).

B. R. Ballinger, 'The Patient's View of Psychiatric Treatment', *Health Bulletin*, vol. XX1X no. 4 (October 1971) pp. 192–6.

Virginia Beardshaw, *Conscientious Objectors at Work – Mental Hospital Nurses – A Case Study* (Social Audit, 1981) p. 81.

Virginia Beardshaw, 'Aiming to be Less of a Client, More of an Ally', *The Health Service Journal* (1 September 1988) pp. 994–6).

Peter Beresford and Suzy Croft, 'Language for Service Users', *Social Work Today* (11 August 1988).

G. E. Bermak, 'Do Psychiatrists Have Special Emotional Problems?', *American Journal of Psychoanalysis* 37(1977) pp. 141–6.

William Bingley and Ronald Lacey, *Inside Out* (MIND, 1988).

Anthony Bird, Jenny Cobb and Mohammed T. L. Walji, 'Increased Patient Participation Using an Extended Consultation: An Inner City Study', *Journal of the Royal College of General Practitioners* (May 1988) pp. 212–14.

A. and D. Brandon, *Consumers as Colleagues* (MIND, 1987).

David Brindle, 'The Resounding Call of the Whistle-Blower Nurse', *The Guardian* (4 July 1990).

British Association of Social Workers, *Clients are Fellow Citizens* (May 1980).

British Medical Association, *Handbook of Medical Ethics* (1982).

British Medical Association, *Philosophy and Practice of Medical Ethics* (BMA, 1988).

M. Brost and T. Johnson (eds), *Getting to Know You – One Approach to Service Assessment and Planning for Individuals with Disabilities* (Madison, Wisconsin Council on Developmental Disabilities, 1982).

J. P. M. Campbell and J. G. R. Howie, 'Involving the patient in reporting adverse drug reactions', *Journal of the Royal College of General Practitioners* (August 1988, pp. 370–1).

Franklin D. Chu and Sharland Trotter, *The Madness Establishment*, Ralph Nader Study Group report on the National Insitute of Mental Health (Grossman, 1974).

Nicki Cornwell, 'On Record and Open to Question', *Social Work Today* (18 January 1990).

Department of Health, *Working for Patients* (1989) paragraph 1.13.

Department of Health and Welsh Office, *Code of Practice on the Mental Health Act, 1983* (HMSO, 1990).

Paul Dolan, 'Access to Personal Files: A Practical Guide to the Act', *Social Work Today* (30 March 1989).

Ronald Dworkin, 'Autonomy and the Demented Self', *The Millbank Quarterly*, vol. 64, supplement 2 (1986).

Annie Faulkner, 'How to catch the CAB', *Nursing Times* (1 October 1986).

Grant Gillett, 'Informed Consent and Moral Integrity', *Journal of Medical Ethics* 15(1989) pp. 117–23.

Larry Gostin, *A Human Condition*, vol. 1(MIND, 1975) pp. 109–10.

Janet Gregory, *Patients' Attitudes in the Hospital Service*, Royal Commission on the NHS (HMSO, 1978, pp. 103-4).

James D. Guy, *The Personal Life of the Psychotherapist* (John Wiley, 1987).

V. Herbert, 'Informed Consent – A Legal Evaluation', *Cancer* 46, 4(1988) pp. 1043.

Roger Higgs in Michael Lockwood (ed.), *Moral Dilemmas in Modern Medicine* (Oxford Univ, 1985) p. 102.

John Illman, 'Medical Record You Can't Forget', *The Guardian* (5 Jan. 1990).

F. J. Ingelfinger, 'Informed (But Educated) Consent', *New England Journal of Medicine*, 28(1972) pp. 465–6.

Richard M. Jones, *The Mental Health Act 1983 with annotations by Richard M. Jones* (Sweet & Maxwell 1982, p. 58).

Elaine Kempson, *Informing Health Consumers* (College of Health, December 1987).

Stuart A. Kirk and Herb Kutchins, 'Deliberate Misdiagnosis in Mental Health Practice', *Social Science Review* (June 1988) pp. 223–37.

L. S. Kubie, 'Pitfalls of Community Psychiatry', *Archives of General Psychiatry*, 18(1968) pp. 257–66.

Lambeth MIND, *Thoughts of Home – The Views of Your Consumers* (245a Coldharbour Lane, London SW9 8RR, 1988).

The Lancet, 'Write for Your Patient' (1989) no. 1, p. 1175.

Jeremy Laurance, 'Silencing the NHS', *New Statesman/Society* (10 June 1988).

Charles W. Lidz *et al.*, *Informed Consent: A Study of Decision Making in Psychiatry* (Guilford Press, 1984).

J. G. Looney *et al.*, 'Psychiatric Transition from Training to Career: Stress and Mastery', *American Journal of Psychiatry*: 137(1980) pp. 32–5.

Dave Lowson, 'Successful Workers?', *IAMHW Bulletin*, no 8 (1989).

R. Masnik, 'Telling a Schizophrenic Patient His Diagnosis', *American Journal of Psychotherapy* 18(3) (1974) pp. 452–7.

MIND, *Understanding Caring* (1989).

MIND/Roehampton Institute, *People First* (1990).

Ralph Nader (ed.), *The Consumer and Corporate Accountability* (Harcourt Brace, 1973).

David Neville and Dick Beak, 'Solving the Case History Mystery', *Social Work Today* (28 June 1990).

Florence Nightingale, *Notes on Nursing* (London, 1859).

Clifton Perry, 'A Problem with Refusing Certain Forms of Psychiatric Treatment', *Social Science and Medicine*, vol. 20, no. 6 (1985) pp. 645–8.

Presidents Commission for the Study of Ethical Problems in Medicine and Biomedical and Behavioural Research, *Making Health Care Decisions* vol. 1, Report (October 1982) ch. 5.

Lydia Sinclair, 'A Plea to Access to Personal Files', *Social Work Today* (17 Nov. 1986).

Helen Smith, 'Collaboration for Change', in David Towell, Sue Kingsley and Tom McAusland (eds), *Managing Psychiatric Services in Transition* (King's Fund College, 1989).

Kathryn M. Taylor, 'Telling Bad News: Physicians and the Disclosure of Undesirable Information', *Sociology of Health and Illness*, vol. 10, no. 2 (June 1988).

Richard Titmuss, *Essays on the Welfare State* (Allen & Unwin, 1958) p. 127.

Henry Walton (ed.), *Education and Training in Psychiatry* (King's Fund, 1986) p. 54.

World Health Organisation and United Nations Children's fund, *Primary Health Care – International Conference on Primary Health Care*, Alma Ata, USSR (Geneva, WHO and UNICEF, 1978).

World Health Organisation, *Consumer Involvement in Mental Health and Rehabilitation Services* (Division of Mental Health, WHO, 1989).

6

Adventurous Listening

On its own, information is not enough. It resembles an off-peak electric radiator system in which energy goes only one way – from the main grid into the individual radiators. It discharges heat steadily during the daytime, gradually running down towards nightfall and then stores up overnight. Using the same model, information can flow only from the service system to the users.

Systems can devalue the staff as well as users. They can feel worthless, that no one acknowledges their skill and experience. Staff who feel powerless can hardly share power with users. In such situations, it easy to scapegoat 'difficult' individuals, whether staff or users, and avoid looking at the real culprits – oppressive structures. Derek Thomas comments about mental handicap services: 'In meeting the needs of one devalued exploited group (the mentally retarded), we created another devalued exploited group (residential staff members)' (quoted in A. and D. Brandon, 1988).

To have real influence, the wisdom and experience of patients must be valued along with that of the professionals. Feedback to the systems is crucial for the improvement of skills and the relevance of treatment. If users are to play a serious part in restructuring systems and re-shaping services, they must have influence and responsibilities. This means effective consultation channelled upwards towards senior managers who make policy and distribute scarce resources. Channelling upwards towards powerful managers is always more difficult than channelling downwards.

Recently, we did some evaluation training in a psychiatric service, paid for and approved by the Health District. We were training staff in monitoring and evaluation. I and three nurses on the course talked to staff and users in a day centre to gain their views on quality. At mid-morning, the consultant psychiatrist

98

arrived and asked the charge nurse who we were and what we were doing. He was reminded of information provided to all staff the previous week. He instructed the charge nurse that under no circumstances were we to talk to any of his patients. So much for feedback and user power!

Users' views have played little part in the formulation of policies on mental illness services. Cohen writes:

> the past twenty years have seen eight official reports on the special hospitals in general or Broadmoor in particular. No ex-patient has ever been asked to contribute to these reports by sitting on committees that drew them up, and, as far as I can make out, only one ex-patient ever gave evidence to any of them. The reports did not search out the patients' views. Psychiatric patients, in general, are not supposed to know what is best for them. (Cohen, 1981)

We are just reaching a period in our psychiatric history where that seems rather bizarre. It is like trying to find out the quality of a supermarket and interviewing only the management and staff and no shoppers.

Treatment of mental illness has been primarily about what psychiatric 'experts' say and decide. The user is seen as damaged and devalued, at least during his time as a patient. He is not able to be a full partner or even a full citizen. He possesses little 'insight' into his condition. His role is defined by powerful others, most of whom spend little time with him or his relatives. He is seen as crazy, disturbed, immature, child-like and unreliable, with very little to contribute and much to take and be given. If he is critical, there is always the 'difficult' patient syndrome; it is a symptom of his mental illness, or he becomes a general nuisance and acquires the shopping-bag term 'psychopath'. It is entirely possible to have an unresolved Oedipus Complex, all manner of personal difficulties, and still be right!

It is true that some users are difficult. An International Hospital Federation study recognises that soberly: 'There are some patients whose views are particularly difficult to obtain, or who are often conveniently forgotten, the mentally ill and children' (IHF, 1988). However, that difficulty is hardly limited to them. We have our share of strange and uncommunicative staff!

I recall a particular Regional Medical officer on hearing the argument for participation by mental illness patients in policy-making and management express red-faced indignation along the lines of 'It's almost impossible to get the professional psychiatric staff to be sensible never mind involving crazies in making decisions. That would push everything towards anarchy.' Professionals like him believe that the task of users is to be treated, do as they are told passively with few questions, take the drugs prescribed and get right out of the service, preferably back into profitable employment and a secure family and never return.

The professionalised view is that doctors, nurses and others decide on the nature and policies of mental illness services. That means taking major responsibilities and bossing people about. Patients learn to collude in this process. Long-stay patients in our Prestwich mental hospital study saw themselves as 'followers', 'mediocre', 'looked after', 'thought for', with little control over their lives'. A major strategy lay in keeping their heads down. Staff were seen as 'leaders', 'protecting patients', 'more responsible', 'mobile with much over their lives particularly during their time off'. One patient saw himself as surviving by pretending he had not been 'demobbed' and was still in the services (A. and D. Brandon, 1987) .

Consider this passage regarding medical intervention (one hopes this is an extremist position): 'Modern medical science is efficacious and therefore the recommendations made by a medical practitioner (in collaboration with the patient) will, if adhered to, benefit the patient'; and 'the practitioner is an expert on matters of health and illness by virtue of his/her special command over medical knowledge' (DiMatteo and DiNicola, 1982, pp. 250).

From this base, it is argued that:

Non compliance interferes with the practitioner's therapeutic efforts, and in addition to exacerbating the already poor health of the patient, prompts the practitioner to order a renewed round of diagnostic evaluation and/or to prescribe another (second-choice) regimen. These maneuvers are likely to bring discomfort to the patient and confusion to the practitioner. They enhance the cost, risk, and uncertainty of the patient's case. If the patient remains ill and the practitioner continually frustrated, the therapeutic relationship is likely to be jeopardised. (DiMatteo and DiNicola, 1982, p. 3)

DiMatteo and DiNicola dismiss completely the uncertainties of medicine, calling it a science rather than an art. What happens if the various medical practitioners, to say nothing of other professionals, disagree over treatment: does the poor patient spectate from his ringside seat while they slug it out? What happens if the patient is utterly compliant and the treatment does not work? What happens about conflict, incompetence and malice in medicine? They dismiss any expertise of the patient in knowing about her unique body and life. They reject wholeness in favour of individual lesions and clusters of symptoms – alleopathic rather than homeopathic medicine. They ignore Hippocrates' wise counsel 'The nature of the person is more important than the nature of the disease.'

By posing 'compliance or non-compliance' or rather obedience to medical instructions as the major issue, they miss the point. It has nothing much to do with professionals getting patients to do what they are told. Here are two ordinary people, neither of them walking six inches above the ground and both without harps, engaging in a complex transaction about 'sickness' and treatment. One is usually in pain and suffering; the other may have relevant skills and knowledge. During that transaction they contribute different perspectives and may disagree. Neither tries to manipulate the other to win control. Instead, they move gently towards compromises and agreements. They move towards sharing information and respect for each other's position. They are humble rather than arrogant: aware of what they do not know rather than what they know. In particular, the practitioner should respect the autonomy of the patient and learn something of his/her whole life.

Other medical practitioners rationalise the manipulation of the 'unco-operative patient' rather more subtly:

The notion of the therapeutic alliance is between the therapist and the healthy part of the patient against the illness that resides within the patient . . . Efforts directed towards involuntary treatment should be candidly described in terms of their purpose in serving the patient's interests, even though they are contrary to the patient's wishes. The clinicians must take an unequivocal stand against psychotic distortion of the treatment situation and continue to maintain a realistic view of the patient's medical needs. (Gutheil and Mills, 1982)

Here the metaphor is of a complex duel. The physician is the only person competent to understand the nature of the conflict.

Gillett raises the question of how patients can 'make things impossible by acting on fixed or superstitious opinions or by failing to participate responsibly' for medical practitioners (Gillett, 1989). Have they a monopoly on fixed opinions? What about the role of medicalised superstitions from the masturbation theories of the nineteenth century to the pick-you-up tonics of the 1950s?

The central element of this whole conundrum is, when can it be reasonable and desirable to intervene against another's wishes?:

the psychiatric patient who refuses that therapy necessary for competency with the goal of becoming incompetent denies the capacity necessary for the exercise of the right of autonomy. Such a patient, therefore, freely abnegates his status as an autonomous being. But since one does not have the freedom to abnegate one's autonomy for its own sake, no violation of patient autonomy is perpetrated by not allowing the psychiatric patient to refuse the medications necessary for autonomous behavior. Nevertheless, there may be *other* reasons, e.g. fear of deleterious iatrogenic effects of the . . . drug regime, which might justify the presently drug-induced competent patient's refusal of that therapy essential for continued competency. (Perry, 1985)

Juxtapose that argument with 'I think that the richness of my pre-injection days, even with the brief outbursts of madness, is preferable to the numbed cabbage I have become' (Westcott, 1979).

Why concentrate exclusively on the damaged and sick parts of the patient? What about our own sick parts projected into professional roles, particularly those of paternalism, and the fear of chaos? What about our attempts to control interviews: our attempts to feel good; to treat ourselves at the expense of others? Are these issues to be ignored?

In any transaction, we need to examine both the 'sickness' and 'health' which each brings to the meeting. What do terms like 'realistic', 'competent' and 'objective' really mean or are they simply a broom to sweep away a whole rubbish pile of difficult ethical and psychological issues? Are we professionals deemed inherently competent to manage the lives of those who are poor and sick and, if so, on what grounds and wherein lies our relevant training and expertise ? And what about wounded healers, nurses, psychiatrists and social workers like myself who become mentally ill. Do we journey gradually or suddenly from one framework of competence/incompetence to another?

Many arguments simply rationalise autocracy in professional practice. 'When I raised a query about my drugs she silenced me: "I prescribe the drugs here; I am the doctor and I am wholly responsible for your drugs." Again when I quoted to her something the clinical psychologist had said concerning the possibility of discharging me she said "I'm in charge of your case and I take all the decisions about your discharge"' (Sutherland, 1977) This patient was a Professor of Psychology who had become extremely depressed. Not much space for co-operative discussion here!

Kay and Legg summarise the experience of some former psychiatric patients who were bossed about:

> Patients had little involvement, choice or control in the discharge decisions, or in arrangements for rehousing and for day care; most received no practical advice or information on welfare benefits or medication before discharge . . . There was consistent evidence of better treatment for those selected by professionals as the 'deserving' mentally ill; these people experienced more preparation, discussion and choice and more later moved to specialist or supported accommodation . . . Although the majority preferred living outside hospital, 80 per cent were dissatisfied with their current housing; many living in temporary accommodation (emergency homeless accommodation or social service hostels) were critical of the rules, regimes and enforced community; others living in independent housing alone or with their families were particularly concerned about their physical housing conditions. (Kay and Legg, 1986)

They experienced different controls over their lives even outside the mental hospital.

Some professionals use the threat of abandonment to get their way. 'Do what I say or else I won't provide any more services . . .' It is no longer a recommendation but a crude instruction accompanied by sanctions for disobedience. It transforms information and advice into blackmail. It does major injury to any effort to establish an easy and equal relationship between the partners. On the most charitable view, it misunderstands fundamentally the nature of the practitioner/patient relationship, outside the compulsory provisions laid down by the law. Less charitably, it understands that nature rather too well and exploits it. The patient is a free agent who comes or is brought for 'advice' from the 'consultant'. He listens to advice and decides whether to take it or not. He should be able to return and take 'advice' again as and when he chooses. That is the essential meaning of the term. The practitioner can express exasperation that the advice is rejected and that the patient sometimes gets into increased difficulties but threats should be avoided.

I came across several cases of both threatened and actual medical abandonment whilst working with North West MIND. One nurse, who worked in a General Hospital, came to see me about his wife:

> She has been chronically depressed these last few years. I have been very worried about her. We went to see the consultant psychiatrist who advised us that as anti-depressants hadn't helped, it was time to give ECT a try. He suggested six sessions of shock treatment. We went home and considered it. Neither of us was keen. We went again to see the consultant and expressed our reservations. He said that if we refused advice about ECT he would refuse to see us any more. So we agreed to the course of six shocks. It didn't really help. I felt angry that we had been blackmailed, especially as it would have been very difficult to get someone else to treat her in our town.

Most reputable authorities hold more enlightened views about professional advice. The Council of Europe recommended 'a shift from the patient's compliance to co-operation between the patient and health care workers as essential' (Council of Europe, 1980). This notion of an equal partnership is an increasingly popular one, at least in theory.

We need more people to complain and to have higher expectations. 'Difficult patients' make more work for front-line staff even
if they may ultimately improve the service quality. Junior staff are
preoccupied with what happens right now. Dissident patients are
constantly pointing out the considerable gaps between what is
promised or can be reasonably expected and what is delivered on
the ward or in the day centre. They don't do as instructed. They
ask lots of questions which absorb time and effort, taking staff
away from whatever their 'real' work is. The services try to knock
the dissident energy out of both staff and patients, so they become
more bovine and malleable. 'Hospital makes you fat, lazy, stupid
and dependent like a child.' 'The trouble is that services are
planned without any consultation with the people who use the
service. Changes in the service are made without really telling
anyone' (Resettlement Group, 1987). Complaints about being
treated like children are common.

Enoch Powell, one-time Minister for Health, put it eloquently
and elegantly:

Traditionally, the hospital patient has been lucky and glad to be
looked after, whether an out-patient, casualty, or in-patient. The
historical origins of the hospitals are either charity, religious or
secular, or the Poor Law authorities. These origins are still
detectable in the attitude of hospital staffs to their patients:
anyone who questions this can verify it for himself unless he is
exceptionally fortunate, by simply taking a seat for an hour or
two on benches in an out-patient or reception department. The
patient and the patient's relatives are face to face not with the
doctors but with the panoply of an institution, physical,
corporate and social. All the romance, wonder and terror of
modern medical science is associated with the hospital and its
deep recesses: the hospital has prestige and inspires awe. For
good measure, the hospital patient is often for one reason or
another helpless. (Powell, 1975).

He conveys that sense of awe that we often have in dealing with
mysterious institutions like hospitals, high courts and cathedrals.
When we feel completely overwhelmed and ignorant, self advocacy
becomes extremely difficult.

Few mental illness professionals who have not been patients, particularly on the psychiatric side, fully understand that. In psycho-dynamic terms, doctors and their surrounding institutions attract a huge range of projections from the relatively powerless patients. That is one reason why hospital dramas are so popular on TV. They provide embroidery for the fantasies of hospital users about the mysterious activities of staff. Few dramas give the patients much more than a peripheral role. The unctious smells from the workhouse, the expected role of the good pauper/patient to be uncomplainingly grateful for what little you get is still part of the unconscious expectations of many services. He or she does not expect to be listened to – never mind be heard as well.

The nurse took my tablets off me and made a final brisk squiggle on her clip-board. "There's a list of mealtimes and a washing-up rota on the notice board upstairs" she said. "Toilets and bathroom down to the corridor on the left. If you want a bath ask a nurse for the taps." It was as simple as that. Ten minutes ago I had been a responsible adult. Now I was a patient in a psychiatric unit and had to ask for the bath taps. It all seemed unreal, like a scene from a play except that I was alone in a room in a psychiatric unit and the play did not end. (Fiona, 1981)

She was reduced to the status of a child from the role of a responsible senior hospital social worker with a university degree and post-graduate professional qualification which she had held only half an hour before. As a surrogate child she was infinitely more pliable and malleable. Her important tasks now were: washing up with others, eating, toileting and having a bath, but only with permission from those set in power over her.

Ian Kelly spent months as a psychiatric patient in the Tooting Bec mental hospital in south London, receiving treatment for severe depression. He later killed himself (Hicks, 1989). He wrote a sensitive and valuable account of his valiant attempts at fostering consultation among fellow patients:

During my last weeks in hospital, I tried to persuade other patients that we should hold meetings to discuss issues on the ward. It was already a progressive ward. Every Friday there was a meeting of patients and nurses. Some patients would say they were feeling well, others would say the food was bad. The nurses would say that too many teabags were being taken from the kitchen. This was the patients' meeting.

I thought there was more to patients' rights. I had been willingly placed on a three day section order, which meant that I had to remain in hospital and accept any medication offered. But when I became a voluntary patient once more, I regained the right to refuse medication. One nurse did not know that I had come off section. She did not like me discussing nurses and doctors with other patients. She asked me to take a tranquilliser called largactil. There is no difference between largactil and a mallet. Both knock you out. I refused the treatment.

The incident made me angry. After talking to other patients, I suggested an agenda for a patients' rights meeting. One item was 'the rights of voluntary patients'. The nurse who liked largactil did not like this. She tore the agenda down. I put up another copy and the meeting went ahead.

The first few meetings were not a success. Most discussions were about property and food disappearing. Some patients were critical of the agenda that had been forced on them. They were right, I admitted later. Eventually it was agreed to use the suggestions list and finish with a round-robin discussion. It worked fine. Many comments were negative, but the patients no longer seemed afraid to talk. Often patients would just thank the nurses for what they had decided. Some nurses could not understand this. Why discuss something that had already been decided? They did not consider the patients' view to matter. (Kelly, 1988)

Notice the familiar processes in this account. The nurses raised the issue of the excessive use of teabags in the kitchen, not the most cosmologically significant of issues but safe. In the staff-led meetings the patients are encouraged to whinge about a narrow range of items like food, the ward, Christmas decorations and the annual charabanc trip to Worthing. Patients steer or are steered away from difficult areas like staff–patient relationships and the use of medication and ECT. It is process made famous by *One Flew over the Cuckoo's Nest*.

When a patient starts to widen the debate, there is often some professional who gets defensive. The patient is usurping the dominant role of the professional. Some nurses fight back, trying to undermine the delicate growth of user autonomy. Tearing down notices written by patients, usually not properly authorised by the hospital authorities anyway, is a common response. When a fruitful atmosphere is provided, the trivia continues for some time, and then talk about riskier themes can flow. Staff also need support and training about the importance of the whole process that patients are going through – re-owning their autonomy. Staff can easily feel threatened and disturbed and feel that their authority, roles and livelihood are all under attack.

I recall an excellent meeting involving long-stay mental illness patients discussing their 'decanting' from one ward to another for re-decoration purposes – the ward not the patients. They were angry and animated. They protested about the proposed disruption. They felt powerful. On the way out to the car park, the charge nurse accompanied me. He was furious both with the patients and with me. 'You were inciting them to a near riot. They've never been that upset before. You've upset them. Anyway it doesn't matter,' he muttered darkly. I asked for further clarification. 'Well, what they decide doesn't matter. They're only patients. Only the staff have full information and understand all of what is going on. They must make the really important decisions.' This is the helicopter position. Patients walk whilst professionals fly like Icarus!

In an early meeting on self-advocacy, this staff group had complained bitterly that patients never talked about anything important in staff-led meetings. They were boring. Yet when an outsider ran the meetings and patients began complaining fluently about restrictive regimes on the ward leading to unnecessarily early getting up times, staff complained about a near riot!

What ingredients are needed to foster real consultation? MIND outlines eight principles for a comprehensive mental health service which include the following: 'value the client as a full citizen with rights and responsibilities, entitled to be consulted and to have an active opportunity to shape and influence relevant services, no matter how severe his or her disability; aim to promote greater self determination of the individual on the basis of informed and realistic choice' (MIND, 1983).

Wolfensberger writes about cultivating an atmosphere of 'realistic optimism'. Staff and services must develop and nurture a culture which recognises the value and wisdom of users. They must see them as able to make unique and important contributions (Wolfensberger, 1971). One crucial ingredient in this atmosphere for Perske is the 'dignity of risk' – an antidote to suffocating protection:

> Many who work with the handicapped, impaired, disadvantaged, and aged are overzealous in their attempts to 'protect', 'comfort', 'keep safe', 'take care', and 'watch'. Acting on these impulses, at the right time, can be benevolent, helpful, and developmental. But if they are acted upon exclusively or excessively, without allowing for each client's individuality and growth potential, they will overprotect and emotionally smother the intended beneficiary. In fact, such overprotection endangers the client's human dignity, and tends to keep him from experiencing the risk-taking of ordinary life which is necessary for normal human growth and development. (Wolfensberger, 1971, pp. 194–200)

Responsible risk taking is vital. Our vast health and social service bureaucracies discourage it. They like things done according to the book. They hate spontaneity, fun and surprises. How can we grow except by taking risks and sometimes falling down on our faces? The nature of the risk means that there is always a chance of failure. The alternative is suffocation by over-protection. We all learn through errors of judgement and from seeking out remedies and help. The whole process of learning is important, not some easy attainment of an externally imposed goal.

Staff must listen to feedback and receive necessary training and support. They also tend to become institutionalised, to identify with the ideology of the service which employs them. Users should be encouraged to comment on the more risky elements of service provision as well as on Christmas decorations and food. Amongst the most valuable criticisms are those which feel most destructive. We can be greatly offended by some comments and take them hurtfully and personally. We must not expect users to come up with easy answers. There are no easy answers in the mental illness services that are not also wrong.

A popular community psychiatric nursing textbook is not entirely enthusiastic about feedback:

Who better than the recipient of a treatment can say how effective it has been? They alone have experienced the treatment event; their comments must have some validity. There is no greater temptation than to ignore the comments of patients, for after all they are the unfortunate sufferers of a mental disorder which must make their judgement suspect! Any untoward comments about a programme can therefore be safely shrugged off as distorted and valueless. This is not necessarily true. (Butterworth and Skidmore, 1981)

They are close to 'damning with faint praise'.
Consider this rather more fulsome and optimistic quote:

How can managers be sure that services are relevant to peoples' needs unless they involve users in planning those services? How can mental health workers assess the quality of their work unless they seek the views of those affected by their work? The mental health field is not one where experts know best. There is no single body of knowledge that informs the service and many different theoretical and practical perspectives are employed to help an individual. Feedback from the point of service delivery is essential to ensure that the individual is benefiting from what is being offered.

. . . There are also what can be loosely termed 'therapeutic' reasons for involving people in planning the services they receive. The experience of mental illness is largely characterised as loss of control, over one's mental state, one's environment, over one's freedom – if sectioned under the Mental Health Act. If contact with mental health workers further limits or prevents people gaining control over their lives, then it challenges the legitimacy of the service. In seeking to help people re-establish control over their lives, the relationships with workers will be vital in promoting a sense of worth and competence. (Helen Smith, 1988)

Some authorities use questionnaires to discover the experiences of service users. A survey of user satisfaction took place on one ward of the psychiatric unit of a Sheffield district general hospital. Data was collected by questionnaire guided by a number of semi-structured interviews. The information suggested many ways in which the patients' time in hospital could be made more comfortable and relaxed. Areas attracting particular concern were the food, noise, the provision of information, and boredom.

Part of the whole problem is the inevitable resistance of professionals to consumer feedback, with its implications of criticism. However, if the professionals are genuinely concerned about the acceptability and effectiveness of the services they offer, they must be prepared to accept evaluation by the recipients as standard practice . . .

Experience has shown, however, that user evaluation is not accorded a high priority by nursing staff, perhaps because they find it threatening. Patient-only meetings, for example, are likely to generate an atmosphere of mistrust unless the ground rules are established first, i.e. will the ward staff have the opportunity to comment on patients' grumbles before they are taken further?

. . . it must be remembered that patients are passive recipients of a service provided by professionals, and deficiencies will continue until the patients are allowed to take more control of their lives while within the health care delivery system. Also those people involved in consumer evaluation need to be more than academic researchers: they must also actively campaign for their observations to be acted upon. (Shields *et al.*, 1988)

In the improvement of service quality, effective complaints procedures are a vital mechanism. A National Consumer Council survey indicated that the majority of social service departments in England and Wales had no formal procedures covering all areas of personal social services (National Consumer Council, 1986). A report done by Sheffield University concluded that complaints procedures in social services departments were 'woefully inadequate' (Lewis *et al.*, 1987).

The National Consumer Council and the National Institute for Social Work point out (Berry and Doyle, 1988) that complaints procedures are especially necessary when departments are quasi monopolies. 'Unlike the consumer of private sector services, however, social services clients have little freedom to take their custom elsewhere. This lack of consumer power becomes even more apparent when there is a shortage of resources and when the clients are poor. Complaints arise which cannot be solved by simply changing supplier' (ibid, p. 4). 'Social service users are often such because they cannot exercise the conventional freedom of consumers' (Jowell, 1988).

Berry and Doyle outline some basic principles:

> The purpose of complaints procedures is to protect the rights of clients. Access to procedures should be simple, speedy and comprehensible. Even when social work actions result in the removal of some rights, clients retain the rights to be heard, to be given information and to understand what is happening to them. Clients have a right to complain and to receive redress. Complaints procedures are at the end of a process which includes the provision of information about services, and about powers and duties, as well as the creation of systems of accountability.
>
> Good client care begins with good staff care. Staff cannot be expected to provide a better service for their clients than they themselves receive.

They suggest as good practice:

> formality; independence; staff involvement; training; involvement of elected members; monitoring; information and support for clients through the whole process. 'Client advocacy must be an important aspect of any complaints procedure if clients are to be enabled, and encouraged, to participate in decision making about their lives, and to take up the right to complain' (Berry and Doyle, 1988).

Existing NHS complaints systems are often extremely complex. There are at least seven different complaints routes, depending on which part of the NHS you want to complain about and what the problem is. There is no uniformity between the systems which deal with hospitals, GPs etc. 'Procedures have not been devised in the interests of patients. And there is no mechanism for lessons to be learned from mistakes' (Mason, 1990). What is required is a much more open and uniform system based on users' needs and with clear guidance about access. For example, Leicestershire social services department's 'Children's Rights Service' provides an information guide for young people in care. This has a lively cartoon format to help people make complaints (Oliver, 1990).

The International Hospital Federation stresses the need 'to create an organisational culture in which patient opinion counts'. They warn innovators to expect opposition from staff and also an increase in the numbers of complaints from patients. Staff 'need consumer relations training' and the development of 'skills in asking patients questions to establish what they really think about care received'. They need skills in listening, remembering and explaining, particularly in avoiding jargon. 'They need to be human as well as efficient' (IHF, 1988, p. 22).

The report argues for quality assurance programmes with aims agreed by all staff. This involves a quality circle with real clout to transform users' views into actions. This circle should have a budget, quality indicator levels and continued monitoring. The report also argues for regular patient opinion surveys. 'Most studies give little information about what action should be taken . . . Most service systems for using information are poorly developed and seldom result in action' (ibid, p. 47).

More specific and prescriptive about consultation is the document *Treated Well? A Code of Practice for Psychiatric Hospitals*. It makes good points about effective consultation:

CHOICES – Do professionals listen to and take seriously the wishes of patients? Are the treatment options discussed openly? May people see their own case notes? Are alternative treatments offered? Are people allowed access to a second opinion? . . .

RIGHTS – Is a complaints system established? Is it easy to use? Is information about it given to patients and relatives? Is assistance given in making complaints? Are all complaints investigated? (Good Practices, 1988)

One hopeful sign is the Search conference, developed by the Tavistock Institute of Human Relationships in the 1960s. 'It aims to encourage mutual understanding and co-ordinated action among different groups who share a common concern about a particular issue but approach it from different perspectives.' Search conferences can provide a platform for users to voice their concerns, for example, about community care. A recent conference of users and carers (professionals were deliberately excluded) at the King's Fund concluded:

> Disabled people and their carers knew what they needed from services, but the problem was how to get it; how to get their hands on a share of the power and control over resources which other people currently held. It was often difficult to find the energy to campaign for change: 'fighting is exhausting' someone said, and the sheer effort required for day-to-day living leaves little energy for such activities, though they knew it was often 'those who shouted the loudest who got what they wanted'. (Wertheimer, 1990)

John O'Brien sums up the whole hopeful process of consultation: 'When people not used to speaking out are heard by people not used to listening then real changes can be made' (O'Brien, 1989).

References

Lynne Berry and Nick Doyle, *Open to Complaints – Guidelines for Social Services Complaints Procedures* (NCC and NISW, 1988).

Althea and David Brandon, *Consumers as Colleagues* (MIND, 1987).

Althea and David Brandon, *Putting People First* (Good Impressions, 1988).

C. A. Butterworth and David Skidmore, *Caring for the Mentally Ill in the Community*(Croom Helm, 1981) p. 110.

David Cohen, *Broadmoor* (Psychology News Press, 1981).

Council of Europe, *Final Report on 'The Patient as an Active Participant in His Own Treatment'* (Strasbourg, 1980) recommendation Four.

M. Robin DiMatteo and D. Daniel DiNicola, *Achieving Patient Compliance: The Psychology of the Medical Practitioners Role* (Pergamon, 1982).

Fiona, *MIND OUT* (May 1981).

Grant Gillett, 'Informed Consent and Moral Integrity', *Journal of Medical Ethics*, 15(1989) p. 118.

Good Practices in Mental Health and Camden Consortium, *Treated Well? A Code of Practice for Psychiatric Hospitals* (1988).

Thomas G. Gutheil and Mark J. Mills, 'Clinical Approaches with Patients Who Refuse Medication', in *Refusing Treatment in Mental Health Institutions – Values in Conflict*, eds A. Edward Doudera and Judith P. Swazey (AUPHA Press, 1982).

Cherrill Hicks, 'The Forbidden Face of Violent Death', *The Independent* (14 March 1989).

International Hospital Federation, *And What Would They Know About It?* (1988).

Tessa Jowell in *Whose Social Services? Creating Effective Complaints Procedures in Social Services Departments* (Association of Metropolitan Authorities and the National Institute for Social Work, Nov 1988).

A. Kay and C. Legg, *Discharged to the Community: A Review of Housing and Support for People Leaving Psychiatric Care* (Good Practices in Mental Health, 1986).

Ian Kelly, 'Summer at Tooting Bec', *Marxism Today* (Feb. 1988).

Norman Lewis *et al.*, *Complaints Procedures in Local Government* (Centre for Criminological and Socio-Legal Studies, University of Sheffield, 1987).

Mary-Claire Mason, 'Doctor Knows Best', *New Statesman & Society* (18 May 1990).

MIND, *Common Concern* (1983).

National Consumer Council, *Complaints Procedures in Social Services Departments – A Survey Report* (1986).

John O'Brien, quoted in Nottingham Patients Councils Support Group Information Pack (1989).

Judith Oliver, 'Protecting Procedures', *Social Work Today* (3 May 1990).

Clifton Perry, 'A Problem with Refusing Certain Forms of Psychiatric Treatment', *Social Science and Medicine*, vol. 20, no. 6 (1985) pp. 645–8.

Enoch Powell, *Medicine and Politics, 1975 and After* (Tunbridge Wells, 1976).

Resettlement Group for Psychiatric Users in North Manchester, 'The Patient's Case', *Community Psychiatric Nursing Journal*, vol. 7, no. 6 (Nov/Dec 1987)

P. J. Shields, P. Morrison and D. Hart, 'Consumer Satisfaction on a Psychiatric Ward', *Journal of Advanced Nursing*, 13(1988) pp. 396–400.

Helen Smith, *Collaboration for Change – Partnership between Service Users, Planners and Managers of Mental Health Services* (King's Fund Centre, 1988).

Stuart Sutherland, *Breakdown* (Paladin, 1977), p. 52.

Alison Wertheimer, 'Users Speak Out', *Community Care* (28 June 1990).

P. Westcott, Letter in the *British Medical Journal*, 1(1979) p. 989.

Wolf Wolfensberger (ed.), *The Principle of Normalisation* (NIMR, Canada, 1971).

7

Speaking Out

Advocacy comes in diverse containers. Traditionally, most mental illness professionals, particularly social workers, were seen as having advocacy functions. More realistically, there are full-time independent advocates. Other forms of unpaid advocacy, like citizen and self advocacy, have been encouraged by recent developments among people with learning difficulties.

The advocacy element in mental illness professionals has been loosely defined and conflicts with other responsibilities. For example, 'Social work is a professional helping service that has as its central task assisting people to meet their basic needs by enabling their optimal social functioning' (Siporin, 1975, p. 9). A social worker is

> a spokesman for the needy in our society, particularly for the poor and disadvantaged . . . More recently, this has been referred to as the social worker's *advocacy* role, although with some confusion about its place in an adversary process, and with some neglect about the need for balance between social obligations and the rights of both social workers and clients. To be an advocate is 'to defend, plead for, support, and give evidence for, in an objective, persuasive way'. (ibid, pp. 37–9)

> The social worker is an agent of social control who provides the restructuring, boundary setting, and identity repair needed by personality and social systems. He serves as a social controller, regulator, and limit setter. (ibid, p. 39)

Siporin is guilty of serious understatement in describing this repertoire of roles and many others as 'amazingly extensive' (ibid, p. 41).

Here is the major dilemma. Professionals see themselves as advocates, among many other roles, but are also agents of social control. As well as gatekeepers to resources, they are passport controllers and customs officers, with the power to say who may or may not pass through. Sang comments fiercely that professionals may try to control advocacy. 'Professional involvement is not just inappropriate, it puts any advocacy scheme at risk. Unfortunately, this simple message runs contrary to the vocational ideology of "professional advocacy". How often do we hear the message: "Nurses are the patient's advocates or "Social workers are their client's advocates"?' (Brackx and Grimshaw, 1989).

Allegedly, professionals are flying high over the top of the client seeing his wishes in the context of wider social structures and deeper psychodynamic levels. They decide how much notice is taken of the clients wishes in the context of those forces, both internal and external. Sometimes that can be very little notice, especially when they have clear social control functions. Their training and professional role gives them understanding and responsibilities far beyond the needs of the user. It makes their advocacy role – in defending, pleading for, supporting, and giving evidence for their clients – unreliable, mysterious and lacking in credibility.

Examine these comments:

> although social workers are frequently very active in helping their clients to obtain full rights from other professionals and agencies, they are often reluctant to accept in turn that the same considerations should apply to them, and that, however good their intentions, their actions may not always be beyond question. The Family Rights Group comments: 'a serious flaw in some social workers' thinking . . . is that once they have taken a decision that they consider to be in the best interests of their client, anyone opposing that judgement is deemed to be acting contrary to the best interests of the client'. (Barclay, 12.44)

Professionals attempting an advocacy role are mostly directly employed service providers paid often by the organisation against whom the complaints are being made. In any town in Britain, the vast majority of helping professionals are ultimately responsible at local level to only two people – the Health Services General

Manager and the Divisional Director of Social Services. Few professionals work in either the commercial or not-for-profit sector although the recent Government White Paper *Caring for People* may change that. The advocate nurse, social worker or doctor has an inherent and critical conflict of interest. The alleged oppressor pays their salaries.

Beardshaw illustrates the considerable risks of being a whistle blower advocate from inside the NHS (Beardshaw, 1981). Many nurses who blew the whistle on malpractice in hospitals found themselves the target of attack. They were seen as disloyal in breaking group and professional codes by complaining to outsiders. Few continued working in the service.

Ray Rowden, a young charge nurse working in St Augustine's mental hospital, was part of a group of junior staff whose persistence in reporting the ill-treatment and bullying of patients eventually led to a major regional enquiry. He still remembers the nails embedded in his car tyres, the anonymous telephone threats trying to intimidate him and the faeces which another colleague received through the letter-box from what he calls the 'organised mafia' (Hicks, 1986). More recently, Graham Pink, a charge nurse campaigning against poor quality in the psycho-geriatric service in Stockport where he works, has been suspended (Brindle, 1990).

Very different difficulties arise from relatives acting as advocates. Many parents, wives and husbands have pressed for better conditions for relatives receiving mental illness services often with good effect. Such pressure requires fine judgement for there is a danger that staff and systems may grow resentful, with negative repercussions for the relative.

Often, there are marked differences in perspectives between relatives and users. Even when love and affection is present, relatives and their pressure groups have frequently advocated for security and safety. Not unnaturally, they have been primarily concerned with their own needs rather than with those of their relatives. They have advocated the enlightened asylum option. 'What is much more difficult to create in the community is a sense of safety, and a place where people know they are accepted and have a freedom to be without stigma or ridicule. To recreate that sense of belonging often found within the old style asylums is proving unrealistic in the wider community outside' (Pearson, 1990). That view is a considerable fantasy.

A number of external structures have developed some measure of independent advocacy for patients. The Health Services Commissioner takes up cases, which do not involve matters of professional 'clinical judgement' on behalf of NHS patients. Very few involve the mental illness sector. Only 3 to 4 per cent of the total complaints received by the Local Government Ombudsman are about social services departments (Yardley in Berry and Jones, 1988).

More locally, the Community Health Councils (CHCs) take on userist issues as well as individual cases. Currently CHCs have the right to visit NHS facilities, to receive information on health services activities and to be consulted about changes to services and on future plans (Rathwell, 1990). The Association of Community Health Councils bids for more influence. 'CHCs should have a responsibility for monitoring all of the health care provided in their districts. It also needs to be recognised that they should have the right to visit and inspect services provided outside their area' (ACH, 1989). My own experience is that CHCs, with certain distinguished exceptions, are weakest in working with mental illness service users and those with learning difficulties.

Under the 1959 Mental Health Act, mental health review tribunals were established to decide on the possible discharge of compulsorily detained patients. As there was no easy access to payment a great deal of this work was done by MIND staff and volunteers as well as interested solicitors and social workers. Under the 1983 mental health legislation, such representation is entitled to legal aid and so has been increasingly taken over by professionally trained law staff.

In 1951 the National Council for Civil Liberties (now known as Liberty) published several cases about wrongful detention in mental institutions. Four years later, the King's Fund published a report about cases of custodial neglect and the mass herding of patients in mental institutions (Sedgwick, 1982). In 1971, the MIND campaign about citizens' rights and mental illness began, led by David Ennals, later the Minister of Health.

In the USA action had been more intensive. In 1968, the New York civil liberties organisation began a vast national project of litigation 'to protect and expand the rights of mental patients through court action at both state and federal level' (Sedgwick, 1982, p. 215). Brown notes that litigation in the USA was 'part of the general upsurge of civil liberties activism in the 1960s, largely prompted by the civil rights movement. This provided a backdrop for the formation of patients' rights groups' (Phil Brown, 1985b).

American advocacy practices were influential in Britain through people like Tony Smythe and particularly the American lawyer Larry Gostin, both of whom joined MIND in the early 1970s. Gostin had been a pseudo-patient. Through false papers saying he had been charged with rape, he got himself held in a secure psychiatric hospital. It was a difficult, frightening and turbulent experience. On discharge, he began a series of law suits against the state of North Carolina – all of them successful. The first was brought on behalf of a long-stay patient met inside the institution. The second suit concerned the liberalising of visiting – he had not been permitted to see his family or friends at all. The last suit involved a deal with State officials who agreed that he should draft a statute on compulsory admissions and in-patient rights (Gostin, 1975a).

Gostin and Smythe pioneered ideas of citizens' rights for mental illness patients and made extensive use of the courts, involving patients in the special hospitals for abnormal offenders like Broadmoor and Rampton. Key legal cases, particularly at the European Court of Human Rights, began to clarify what these basic rights were, particularly for detained patients.

Gostin was among the first in Britain to recognise the key role of advocacy. In 1975, he was arguing for an advocacy system which would help 'enforce residents' rights'. 'The term "advocate" is here understood to mean any person working within the system of mental health services to ensure that recipients of those services are not deprived of their rights as citizens under the current or proposed law.' It was important to him that the hiring and supervision of advocates should be undertaken by an agency entirely independent of the government departments. He saw the training of these people, rather like the Dutch Ombudsman, to be in law, medicine, community resources, psychology, bureaucracies, institutional life – with one advocate for each institution (Gostin, MIND, 1975b, p. 131).

Within ten years, Gostin's ideas widened considerably. The advocacy process was now 'one of pleading the cause and/or acting on behalf of mentally ill people to secure the services they require and the enjoyment of their full rights. Advocates may be consumers, volunteers or professionals who act independently. As agents of people with handicaps, they owe them a duty of loyalty, confidentiality and zeal in promoting their cause' (Gostin in Sang and O'Brien, 1984). He recognised the enormous potential for volunteer and even user advocates.

As part of the pressure for new legislation in the late 1970s, to replace the 1959 Act, MIND urged some form of independent advocacy system. In partial response, the 1983 Act set up the Mental Health Act Commissioners. The 92 commissioners have special responsibilities to oversee the rights of detained patients. The recently published Mental Health Act Commissions code of practice has seven broad principles, which include: respect for individual qualities; needs fully taken into account, even if not met; self-determination and personal responsibility promoted to greatest extent consistent with needs and wishes; as fully involved as practicable and consistent with needs and wishes, in formulation and delivery of care and treatment (Department of Health, 1990). One major criticism is that these principles have no direct legal force (Carson, 1990).

MIND's development of formal legal advocacy work and extensive rights campaigns spawned a widespread interest in the voluntary sector. Robson notes:

17 legal advocacy projects based in psychiatric projects. The majority of their work tends to be concentrated on patients' money and cash benefits. Whilst most are independent they tend to be seen as part of the hospital services – something compounded by their work with both users and staff – and on the whole tend not to take action against staff or the hospital, but simply advise people of the appropriate complaints procedure and provide outside help if necessary. (Barker and Peck, 1987)

That these limitations are well founded is illustrated by the advocacy service in Springfield psychiatric hospital:

The Project was initially set up as a sub office of the Wandsworth Legal Resource Project, a local law centre, although the management function was effectively delegated to the Project's own Management Committee from the very beginning . . .

Litigation against the hospital was excluded from the remit of the project. Hospital Managers were present on the project management committee. Over 85 per cent of the problems dealt with by the Project were in areas other than mental health – housing and welfare benefits particularly. (King's Fund, 1986; and in GPMH, 1986)

A report on the similiar Mapperley psychiatric hospital project in Nottingham shows that only 7 per cent of enquiries were about mental health issues (Barker and Peck, 1987).

A major influence in formal advocacy comes from Holland. Currently, there are thirty-one 'patients' advocates' (*Patientenverstrouwenspersoon* – literally meaning 'patients' confidant') attached to psychiatric hospitals. In the 1970s, some hospitals had already appointed an ombudsman who could deal with patients' complaints. In January 1980, a committee with representatives of the mental hospitals, the patients unions and the medical inspectorate of the government, formulated the duties of a patient advocate, recommending that they should operate and be financed completely independently of the hospital administration.

In 1981 an independent foundation was set up with the Dutch government's approval. The Board of the National Foundation for Patients Advocates included representatives from psychiatric hospitals and patients with some independent members. The government obliged all psychiatric hospitals to contribute a limited amount annually to the foundation. Appointments of advocates were made on the basis of an agreement drawn up between the national foundation and the particular hospital. The advocates are employed by the foundation in Utrecht and not by individual hospitals. This removes the major conflict of interest which social workers, for example, face in pressing for a client's rights.

Advocates in Holland have a common training period, a published manual, standardised duties and working methods. The national bureau advises and supports them through difficult situations. The emphasis lies on being the adviser/voice of the individual patient. Dangers lie in the creation of yet another profession with the grand seduction of career opportunities and higher salaries, all pulling them back towards agency function. Another problem is that the necessary focus on individual complaints may not lead to rectifying major structural weaknesses in the system. The focus by advocates on the individuality of complaints and the preoccupation of the *Clientenbond* (the mental patients based in each hospital) with structure can lead to serious tensions.

The advocate aids the mental illness patient in seeking his rights in three ways: she assists in finding solutions to his complaints, she informs the patient concerning his rights and looks into relevant structural shortcomings within the hospital. Advocates do not make impartial rulings: their task is to side with the patient. They visit all the hospital wards regularly and have access to relevant files.

The Netherlands Institute of Mental Health showed in a 1983 study that about 40 per cent of complaints to patients' advocates relate to involuntary commitment and forms of pressure from staff whilst in hospital. Other complaints are about the nature of treatment or about inadequate explanations; lack of attention from staff; staff discourtesy; as well as more general legal matters relating to housing and work outside hospital (Jensen and Pederson, 1985).

One danger of full-time professional advocacy, both in Holland and Britain, is to 'own' the whole process. 'Professionals conceptualise advocacy in such a way as to maintain dominance and increase the use of that profession's services. Lay political participation is mitigated by the use of the professional as the essential intermediary between the individuals or groups with political problems and the formal policy-making process' (Milner, 1985).

Bean makes useful points about this process:

There is an obvious tendency therefore to see rights as being synonymous with patients' care so that more and more rights are equated with similiar advances in care . . . this is entirely correct – at least as far as it goes. For it is clear that a certain level of rights and certain types of rights are central to any care system – mental patient or otherwise. The problems arise, however, when we ask questions about the limitation of rights – or rather if there are limits and if so what are they? And whether those limits are identifiable and whether at a certain point the growth of rights can ever have a harmful effect on the quality of care. Or whether it matters whether the promotion of rights enforced by (say) lawyers are less or more important than those enforced by lay people. (in Barker and Peck, 1987)

In Britain, there has been a positive explosion in unpaid advocacy particularly among people with learning difficulties. In mental illness, that process has been more recent and considerably slower. MIND's statement on advocacy in 1982 contained no reference to advocacy by users. It saw MIND and its local associations speaking out for them (Hebditch, 1982). The Good Practices in Mental Health advocacy information pack (GPMH, 1986) was entirely about paid/professional advocacy or volunteers giving advice on welfare rights. There is no mention of either self or citizen advocacy.

One enormous encouragement to the whole unpaid advocacy movement was the Disabled Persons (Services, Consultation and Representation) Act 1986. Section 1 describes the appointment of representatives, by or on behalf of a disabled person. Disabled people under 16 years old cannot appoint a representative themselves, but this may be done by their parent or guardian or, if they are in care, by the local authority. A parent or guardian may appoint him/herself as their child's representative. Local authorities may appoint representatives for disabled people who appear unable to do so for themselves because of physical or mental incapacity.

The local authority is required to permit an authorised representative to act (at the request of the disabled person) in connection with social service provision, and to accompany the disabled person to any meeting or interview held by or on behalf of the authority linked to that provision. Authorised representatives have rights of access to disabled people at any reasonable time when living in a wide range of accommodation, including private residential homes and nursing homes. These sections have not been implemented, mainly because of financial implications, despite energetic campaigns. However they provide good practice guidelines for health and local authorities.

In the USA, the

Mental Patients Liberation movements provided the first critique of psychiatry to come solely from the perspectives of its clients. Small groups of ex-patients began to assert their anger at being committed for what they saw as minimally deviant acts and then being re-socialised into an institutional lifestyle . . . Mental patients liberation fronts and similiar organisations made their initial appearances with angry denunciations of mental hospital abuses, and sometimes with 'jailbreaks' in which they released friends who had been involuntarily admitted. (Brown, 1985b)

Their publications like *Phoenix Rising*, *Off the Shelf* and *On the Edge* were energetic and often intensely angry. One publication stated bluntly:

Inside mental hospitals, patients are driven crazy and further brutalized. They have no control over their own lives and are constantly at the mercy of staff. One ward had a slogan 'If you're not crazy when you arrive here, you will be before you leave.' Such a slogan is all too true. Although hospitals can represent a sometimes needed 'safe place', they are mostly used to contain, detain, and 'deal with' various social problems. Medication, electroshock, insulin shock, lobotomies and the rigid hierarchical ward systems: these intimidate patients and ensure that the staff has constant and ultimate control. Patients are dependent on staff good will, and on the good will of the relatives who often sent them into the wards. Mental hospitals, especially the large state bins which contain up to 10,000 people, have long since forgone any therapeutic responsibility for their patients; they are instead custodial and detention centres for masses of already oppressed people. (Agel, 1973)

The most recent stimulant comes once more from Holland where mental patients' groups are part of an extensive consumer movement. There are presently 400 patients' organisations with widely differing perspectives, concerned mainly with advocacy, mutual support and the exchange of information. The absence of a common view and co-ordination made it difficult to achieve significant progress until the formation of the National Patients and Consumers Platform (LPCP) in 1982. LPCP represents 135 associations with a total membership of approximately 800,000 people. It campaigns for changes in the health insurance system, statutory regulations for patients' rights, for more privacy and extending rights to complain and participate in service planning and delivery. Underlying these campaigns is LPCP's belief in increased autonomy for patients. It seeks to democratise service delivery systems and to demolish unequal power relationships.

The first Dutch mental patients' group, Pandora, was born in the early 1960s from an advertisement in a weekly newspaper for people who had been psychiatric patients or clients to campaign for better services. The first psychiatric client groups were formed in the early 1970s (Abbott, 1986) and gradually developed into the extensive and influential *'Clientenbond'*, membership of which is restricted to users and ex-users (Haafkens, Nijhof and Van Der Poel, 1986).

Dutch mental illness care is still a closed system with doctors in most key administrative and planning positions (van de Klippe in Jensen and Pedersen, 1985). Mental illness care is often delegated to private agencies which frequently have a Christian denominational background. These agencies have become highly image conscious, producing glossy annual brochures with great sensitivity to press coverage. Quality control systems and userist policies are necessary as part of an overall public relations strategy.

The current law relating to mental illness in Holland is the Lunacy Act of 1884, modified by European High Court judgements in Strasbourg. Repeated attempts to reform and update the century-old legislation have been stillborn. There has been a formidable and fundamental struggle between the various professional groups, in particular the psychiatrists and lawyers and the users' organisations, ever since 1971. The Lunacy Act is mainly about compulsory admission (relatively high at 15 per cent of all admissions). Under the Act a judge decides whether someone should be committed to a mental hospital. Because of its antiquated nature, the Act is mute about the general rights of the mental hospital patient.

Since 1974, there has been a loose consortium of various radical bodies – the *Clientenbond*, a number of solicitors and the Pandora Foundation – pressing for extension of rights of psychiatric patients, often taking hospitals to court. A major turning point was the 1980 manifesto 'Patients Rights in Mental Health Care'. This outlined sixty-four propositions backed by the *Clientenbond* and the Patients Councils. For example, 'Efforts should be made to bring about a rapid termination of the predominant medical and psychological approach in mental health care. More attention should be focussed upon allowing the patients' relatives, friends and work-mates to play a role in the treatment.' 'Efforts should be made to abolish large psychiatric institutions. Mental health care should be shifted to the individual's environment.'

In Britain, advocacy has become an aerosol spray term. 'Today almost anything can be labelled advocacy, even highly traditional services. This is what Wolfensberger refers to as the "tomato sauce" approach to advocacy' (Harris, 1987). The two main kinds are self and citizen advocacy:

Self-Advocacy

The World Federation of Mental Health conference at Brighton in July 1985 gave an important boost to self-advocacy in mental illness. It brought together users from Denmark and Holland with Judy Chamberlin from the USA and committed professionals from Italy. These groups along with a handful of British users and concerned professionals held informal events alongside the pomposity of the large main conference.

Campbell notes that MIND's national conference 'From Patients to People' in November 1985 gave users an opportunity to make presentations in front of the full conference as well as lead workshops. He describes this as 'an event of symbolic importance' (Brackx and Grimshaw, 1989). I gave the final address at this conference, as MIND's only senior staff member/mental illness service user, and vividly recall the excitement and anger in the hall.

Self-advocacy is a simple but powerful idea. Cooper and Hersov define it as

> people being their own advocates and speaking for themselves. That covers a very complex set of concepts. It includes independence, freedom of choice, self- expression, and group awareness. This has major implications for people working with self-advocates. Since most people with learning difficulties are strongly influenced and controlled by parents and professionals, any change towards self-advocacy inevitably means altering the balance of power between the person with the learning

difficulties and parents and staff. So self-advocacy is not only about learning sets of skills, but also changing relationships and attitudes. (Cooper and Hersov, 1986, p. 12)

The Survivors Speak Out (SSO) action pack echoes that approach:

Self-advocacy is about power – about people regaining power over their own lives. The psychiatric system in this country seems peculiarly designed to deny power to those who enter it (or are sent into it) for help. Such powerlessness is then reinforced by the practices and attitudes of the wider society into which the recipients of services eventually emerge. Through self-advocacy, through taking positive action for ourselves, we challenge this process, both by working to change the psychiatric system and by challenging our devalued status in the eyes of the majority of society. (Survivors Speak Out (SSO), 1988)

Traditionally, in Britain, mental illness campaigning has been dominated by voluntary organisations like MIND, speaking out on behalf of a constituency with which it has nebulous contact. Its members are mainly the middle class – a mixture of frustrated mental illness professionals, relatives of patients, and perhaps, last and least influential, direct users.

Slowly MIND has begun to involve users in policy. My impression after working for MIND for eight years is of a considerable amount of internal 'psychiatrism'. Some senior managers were not enthused about working alongside mental patients. Many of more than two hundred local associations, especially the older established ones, had a paternalistic attitude to people with mental illness.

But despite resistances, 'the times they are a'changing'. One concrete indication is the pressure for mandatory users on the executives of MIND local associations. Mike Lawson, a declared user himself, became Vice-Chairman of National MIND several years ago. The MIND consumer network is an initiative to bring together and empower users of mental health services. The Network has a membership of over 450. The newsletter *MINDWAVES* offers a platform for members to express their views, to advertise their activities and make contact with others. It has a channel through elected representatives to a consumer advisory panel, part of MIND's policy-making process (Wallcraft in Winn, 1989).

The North West consumer network is represented on the care committee of Fazakerley Hospital, north Liverpool, and in the planning of access to education courses for ex-patients. It influenced the successful defence of a popular Merseyside day centre threatened with closure (*Consumer Network News*, 1990). Wallcraft says 'People who have been through the psychiatric system are a valuable resource and our experience as ordinary people can help others. We want to make sure that the government provides services that people need instead of just following old patterns and repeating old mistakes' (Winn, 1989). The network has few resources and it is early days to see how serious MIND is about user power.

The work of Good Practices in Mental Health (GPMH) has shifted substantially. Its development team focused on establishing district wide, user-only mental forums. These include the Islington Forum, Lewisham Users Forum and Connections in Harrow. GPMH offers help in applications for funding; training; publicity; gaining charitable status; running workshops, etc. (Halford, 1989).

Self-advocacy groups develop campaigns and services. Their work often mirrors the efforts of major voluntary organisations but on a local basis. The difference is that this campaigning comes directly from the personal experiences of direct service users. The majority of existing groups are alliances of users and workers with a small element of 'carers'. The best known is Survivors Speak Out (SSO), an umbrella organisation formed shortly after the 1985 MIND conference. SSO is moving towards a position of full membership for survivors and associate membership for allies (Campbell, personal communication, 1990). Their regular newsletter tells of different user groups blossoming in many parts of the country. The January 1990 issue contains the addresses of 33 self-advocacy groups, mainly based in the south of England and particularly in the London Boroughs.

One seminal event was the SSO conference in the Derbyshire Peak District in September 1987 where members hammered out a Charter of Needs and Demands:

that mental health service providers recognise and use people's first-hand experience of emotional distress for the good of others . . . A Government review of services, with recipients sharing their views . . . provision of resources to implement self-advocacy for all users . . . facility for representation of users and ex-users of services on statutory bodies, including Community Health Councils, Mental Health Tribunals and the Mental Health Act Commission . . . full and free access to all personal medical records . . . provision of all patients of full written and verbal information on treatments, including adverse research findings. (SSO, 1988).

In March 1989, the newsletter campaigned against the advertising of a newly formed voluntary mental illness organisation, SANE:

AGAINST NEGATIVE STEREOTYPING   There has been a widespread reaction against the SANE (Schizophrenia: A National Emergency) STOP THE MADNESS publicity .campaign, which includes poster slogans emphasising the violent/ alien aspects of 'schizophrenia', e.g. 'He thinks he's Jesus Christ.' 'You think he's a killer.' 'They think he's fine.' Among groups and individuals who have been protesting at the rabble-rousing style of the above has been the London Alliance for Mental Health Action which organised a street theatre demonstration at the site of one of the posters nearby the Imperial War Museum (the old site of the Bethlem Hospital). (Read, 1989–90)

Another important milestone was a meeting in June 1989 at the House of Commons between more than thirty users from as far afield as Scotland and Plymouth with senior Labour Party politicians, including Robin Cook, the Shadow Health Minister. This was the first time a major political party had consulted users on mental illness policy. They made representations under three headings: user involvement in the planning and management of services; types of services; political issues which included minority groups and the ideology of services.

Helen Smith outlines succinctly the diversity of political approaches amongst these self/collective advocacy groups:

Some groups are advocating user-run services and feel their experience of the psychiatric system as being one of disempowerment and restriction of rights . . . Other user groups are asking for involvement in monitoring services, training workers and representation in planning; seeking to influence services at a local level, they are not concerned to be directly involved in managing services . . . Some user groups are asking for changes not directly related to deficiencies in the health system, such as higher benefits or better employment opportunities . . . Other groups still, are asking for better services provided by the psychiatric systems such as improved out-patient facilities; or see their role as supporting other users within the advocacy framework. (Helen Smith, 1988)

There are broadly two different approaches: Separatists and Partnerists.

Separatists are inspired, among other sources, by Judy Chamberlin: 'ex-patients provide support for one another and run the service. All nonpatients and professionals are excluded because they interfere with consciousness raising and because they usually have mentalist attitudes' (Chamberlin, 1988, p. 94). Chamberlin uses the example of the Fountain House project in New York, which began as 'We Are Not Alone' (WANA).

There was a feeling of solidarity and companionship in WANA that deteriorated when the professionals got involved. For a while, the ex-patients continued to run the club. We raised our own money (by holding bazaars, for example), and we voted in new members. But eventually the administrators decided to take that power away from us. Instead of the members deciding who could join, when new people came in they were interviewed by the staff, who decided if they were 'suitable cases'. WANA was unique because patients ran it – that was abolished when it became Fountain House. (from Jordan Hess in Chamberlin, 1988)

Chamberlin notes more recently:

Those groups that did not exclude non-patients from membership almost always quickly dropped their liberation aspects and became reformist . . . group members began to recognise a pattern they referred to as 'mentalism' or 'sane chauvinism', a set of assumptions which most people seemed to hold about mental patients: that they were incompetent, unable to do things for themselves, constantly in need of supervision and assistance, unpredictable, likely to be violent or irrational, and so forth. Not only did the general public express mentalist ideas; so did ex-patients themselves. These crippling stereotypes became recognised as a form of internalised oppression. (Barker and Peck, 1987)

Chamberlin recognises, along with sexism and racism, what she calls 'mentalism'. Most ordinary people grow up surrounded by much negative imagery of 'madness' and develop unreasonable fears of madness. They learn to fear chaotic behaviour in others and going 'mad' themselves, a fear exploited in a thousand Hollywood B movies and ten thousand crass gutter-press headlines. For example, the film, Hitchcock's *Psycho* probably put back the resettlement of mental illness patients twenty years.

Few British groups have taken a separatist line. Among the oldest established was the Mental Patients Union (MPU) formed in March 1973. The MPU charter took a fierce stance. 'Professionals are agents of repression. Professionals make their living out of those who are oppressed. It is a necessary part of their existence that they define their clients as "abnormal" in order to preserve their own "normality", and, therefore, their own financial positions.' (Sedgwick, 1982, p. 227) The charter continued:

Social (and political) deviants are punished for being different from 'normal' people (or attempts to 'rehabilitate' them to 'normality') in a society where normality is to be a robot on a production line; to compete against other human beings in the survival of the fittest; to cope in appalling poverty, begging for social security (social insecurity); and to live in high-rise boxes or rat-infested slums. (Mental Patients Union, 1972)

Partnerists try to establish close relationships between consumers and professional staff. They are not trying to take over anything. They argue that clients/users/patients are really colleagues. Their inherent philosophy is usually based on the ideologies of partnership. In view of the massive imbalance of resources/education/ social status between professionals and users, that is intrinsically a very difficult position.

Most self-help groups, with an advocacy function, fall into this category. Katz and Bender define these groups, of which there are rapidly developing numbers in mental illness, as:

> Voluntary small group structures for mutual aid in the accomplishment of a specific purpose. They are usually formed by peers who have come together for mutual assistance in satisfying a common need, overcoming a common handicap or life-disrupting problem, and bringing about desired social and/or personal change. The initiators and members of such groups perceive that their needs are not or cannot be met by or through existing social institutions. (Katz and Bender, 1976)

Most such groups seek to co-operate with professionals. For example, the Phobics Society states 'We will co-operate with welfare services, local authority services and with other voluntary organisations for the benefit of all phobic persons.' Medical and psychological consultants are represented on the management committee.

The Camden Mental Health consortium produced a report on provision based on a questionnaire to all members. 'Mental Health Priorities in Camden As We See Them – The Consumer Viewpoint' was presented to the authorities and led to involvement in the whole planning process. Campbell notes:

> The real-life experience of service users are facts with their own value. They are not simply concoctions of a fevered imagination. Planners' resistance to written material appears to be weaker than it is to oral or anecdotal evidence, which although it may contain emotional and human impact does not survive easily in a bureaucratic environment. It is difficult but by no means impossible to combine the immediacy of the service users experience with a well ordered and rational argument to achieve a presentation which has human and intellectual impact. This, in essence, is what the consortium has been working towards. (Campbell, 1987)

An impressive example of an advocacy partnership is the Hackney Multi Ethnic Women's Health Project. It emphasises community control over the whole project and a partnership with relevant professionals.

It is not in the direct interest of managers and administrators to promote criticism of the services for which they are responsible. For reasons which are not difficult to understand, NHS managers faced with the prospect of having to provide for black and ethnic minority patients, have preferred to appoint interpreters rather than patient representatives/advocates. The feeling of the Multi Ethnic Women's Health Project . . . is that an advocacy scheme run from within the health service is almost a contradiction in terms and would – very rapidly – become an interpreting service. (Cornwell and Gordon, 1984)

Harris provides a lively account of the development of one local group. The establishing of the forum began in June 1986 arising out of a Good Practices in Mental Health document. The full-time organiser gave talks to user groups and workers and users in both hostels and day centres. That was followed by a poster and leaflet campaign (Harris, 1989). The big step is:

to move from anger at the way you have been treated to negotiate with the professions. Just being angry is destructive but putting forward ideas is constructive, and making demands becomes proactive . . . Professionals are delicate creatures and most are demoralised . . . Groups give credibility to individual voices . . . Users are not as delicate as some think. Staff must, as users have pointed out in Forum meetings, stop interpreting all encounters as a pseudo-therapeutic exercise. If a user has a practical problem it needs a practical solution. They are not displaying another symptom. (Renshaw, 1989)

'Insight', based in Brighton, with many members who are users and ex-users, drafted a Users' Charter to help its work as a mental illness pressure group:

Users should be consulted about decisions affecting their daily lives, especially those involving risk . . . Users should have information and explanation relevant to their individual needs . . . Users should be given an explanation of diagnoses in plain language . . . To know there is a recognised, active and practical complaints procedure . . . Not be destructively labelled by professionals. (Insight, 1990)

Irene Whitehill, a service user, worked with the Newcastle Advocacies Project (NAP) during 1988–9, located in the local mental hospital. This project reflected the tensions and intense difficulties in advocacy:

NAP should never have been set up as single worker project. The intermediary role is often impossible and with limited support is made doubly impossible . . . It soon became evident that the establishment of the legitimacy of NAP within the patient population would be a very slow process. Many patients having become institutionalised, finding it very difficult to speak up for themselves and to trust an advocate to speak up on their behalf . . . Many of the difficulties experienced by the Management Group were due to friction between some service users and members with a professional background . . . From an ideological viewpoint an all user Group with professional advisers would be the most acceptable solution. However, those users associated with NAP were sometimes lacking in confidence and relevant skills. (Whitehill, 1990)

The first months of the pioneering advocacy project in Bellsdyke mental hospital in Scotland also saw important struggles. The advocacy worker Colin Murray writes about encountering 'degrees of hostility, support and acceptance'. Psychiatrists banned the project from the Stirling day hospital.

The very presence of the project has led to a number of spin offs, a number of joint planning groups actively looking for users to attend . . . I cannot share their enthusiasm given the manner in which people are simply picked out and invited. There are a number of questions on this score about incorporating individuals into groups with well-established not to say entrenched agendas with neutralising rather than galvanising effects – a pall of tokenism hangs over these exercises and so called consultation. (Murray, 1990)

This problem of co-option, taking part in planning and management without real influence and impact, is likely to grow. The involvement of users can simply be a public relations gloss.

Citizen Advocacy

In June 1981, the Advocacy Alliance, consisting of five major voluntary agencies – MIND, MENCAP, One-to-One, the Spastics Society and the International Year of Disabled People – was launched following the showing of Nigel Evans's TV documentary *Silent Minority* on appalling conditions in two mental handicap hospitals. The Alliance pioneered citizen advocacy in three such hospitals in the London area (Sang and O'Brien, 1984). Citizen advocacy seeks

> to empower those who have been kept powerless and/or excluded. These aims are shared with many self-help and campaigning organizations, large and small, local and national, throughout the country: the difference is in the method . . . citizen advocacy works by demonstration. Members of devalued groups are put in touch, on a one-to-one basis, with ordinary people who have their own place in the community and who will listen to their point of view, respect their wishes, and stand with them to defend their rights. Individuals who have been stigmatized, ignored and made victims by society are those enabled to assert themselves and become active members of their communities. (National Citizen Advocacy, 1988)

Citizen advocacy is a partnership between an individual who has a disability and another who does not. It is not collective advocacy. It is a match between two people in which the advocate's loyalty is with one specific individual. Schemes are structured to support citizen advocates as unpaid, independent volunteers, each representing only one individual.

To ensure independence, advocates should be:

* supported by, but independent of, the advocacy office. An obligation to submit regular reports for example, may encourage advocates to feel that they are working for the office staff rather than for their partners:
* independent of the agencies and settings which provide services for their partners. Whenever there is a paid service, conflict of interest is inherent and would, for example, certainly arise if the advocate was paid to provide nursing care to their partner or to clean their room.
* independent of the families of their partners in those instances where family interests are different from those of their partners. In this situation, it is vital for the partner to have an advocate who can strengthen their arguments and encourage the family to see their point of view. Close ties with any member of the family might inhibit an advocate.

The principles of citizen advocacy can be applied to anyone whose rights and wishes are ignored and overruled. These principles were developed from the treatment of one group in particular – those people labelled as having learning difficulties who have been incarcerated in institutions, excluded from education, employment, political activity and leisure opportunities, denied access to quite basic human rights and, too often, ridiculed when trying to exercise choices which would be regarded as quite unexceptional in other sectors of society.' (ibid, p. 5)

The citizen advocacy movement is spreading rapidly but not without the chronic problems of remaining independent and inadequate funding. In the USA, Canada and this country most 'partners' are people with physical disabilities or learning difficulties. Very few have a history of mental illness. Carol, who did have experience of mental illness, talks of her meetings with a citizen advocate, Sue:

Meeting Sue for the first time was even worse because I didn't know what she would think of me or if I'd like her. I thought she'd come in and 'sort me out', but she didn't! She asked me to

talk to her [they all do that, don't they!]. I didn't know what to
say, how can you tell a stranger what a mess you're in, but she
said she wasn't interested in that right now, she wanted to know
about ME! I told her there was nothing much to say but a half
hour later I was still going on, talking non-stop (as usual)!

   To cut a long story short we did end up talking about my mess
and Sue helped me work out what 'I' needed to do to sort myself
out. Sue wrote down all the things which were upsetting me and
we talked about which needed to be done first. I'd been seeing
Sue once a week for ages before I told her I couldn't read and
write properly. Her friend Jane is now helping me with this. I
sometimes feel like a five-year-old but it doesn't matter. I'm
happy now, and Sue and her friends don't think of me as being
odd at all. We had some rows over the months but then friends
do that don't they? I'm not saying that all my problems have
gone away, they haven't, but we're working on them ME and
SUE. (Nottingham Advocacy Group, 1988–9)

There has been a tremendous development of both self and
citizen advocacy in the field of learning difficulties particularly
since the formation of the Advocacy Alliance. Many parts of
England have self-advocacy groups for people with learning
difficulties. There are more than 200 affilliated to Peoples First,
the national organisation. More than half Adult Training Centres
(ATCs) have such groups. Most areas plan citizen advocacy offices
with money coming largely from Opportunities for Volunteering
sources.

   Progress in mental illness is much slower and fraught with
difficulties. The citizens advice bureaux, despite some excellent
work, had their wings clipped and struggle for funding. They do
little direct mental illness advocacy and avoid most confrontation.
They are kept out of roles which are bread-and-butter to the Dutch
mental illness advocate. There are still very few self-advocacy
groups and citizen advocates concentrate mainly on people with
learning difficulties and those with physical disabilities. That raises
serious questions.

   Some difficulties arise from ideas and practices spreading from
one client group area to another. New ideas adapt slowly to the
complex entanglement of therapy, treatment and rights, always a
feature of mental illness services. 'Why do you want to insist on

rights when I am trying to make you well and develop your insight?'

Advocacy in mental illness meets very considerable resistances. Professionals get angry at the articulate outsider taking up issues about one of 'their patients'. Most replies to complaints made about poor services received when I was working with MIND were whitewashes. Any investigation was sketchy and the process rarely taken seriously.

Therapy and rights become entangled. I took up the issue of one long-stay patient who alleged he had been attacked by named nurses on the night shift. He showed me the bruises on his shoulders and arms. I wrote a two-page letter to the Health Services Manager. Several months later I received a reply. A long letter gave me, in considerable detail, the social history and psychiatric treatment, including drugs side-effects and ECTs. No mention was made of the alleged attack. The implication was that he was so ill that his allegations were not to be taken seriously. I wrote back that I had not asked for and had no right to such detailed information. I had just been asked to take up allegations of an attack on my client. Would the Manager investigate to see whether such attacks took place? It took another few months to get a response which indicated that the nurses had been questioned and were denying the allegations.

Rose and Black argue powerfully that mental illness treatment should be replaced by models based on advocacy and empowerment and rightly conclude that traditional services would be threatened:

Traditional medicalised models of mental health treatment enhance the position of dominators and exploiters objectively . . . Workers socialized into the power and false charity of medicalised models of care are similarly socialized into dominated power relationships with clients which are dependent upon the client remaining within the crushing, stultifying confines of the mental patient role. When an advocacy/empowerment practice asserts the oppression in that role, the fight for competing legitimacies erupts at every level, beginning with direct face-to-face contact with clients exposed to both orientations and continuing on to homeowners, regulatory agencies and funding systems. The very life of the advocacy/empowerment agency is regularly put on the line, so long as it maintains its espoused commitments. (Rose and Black, 1985, pp. 188–9).

Brown comments on the overall rights scene:

> The patients rights' movement shows that the direct action of a relatively powerless group can have significant effects on overall social policy, even if its success in part depends upon the support of more powerful groups intent on co-option . . . While sympathetic professionals might prefer a more polite form of strategy, it is probably necessary to have the sharp level of criticism and action provided by the patients' movement as a complement to 'mainstream' reform . . . The fact that patients' rights issues are often pressed by a powerless group takes the direction of reform somewhat out of the hands of policy makers and higher-level professionals. This may provide lower-level professionals and paraprofessionals with more impetus to institute change from below. (Brown, 1985b)

References

Max Abbott, 'Patient and Ex-patient Advocacy in the Netherlands: Interview with Wouter van de Graaf', *Community Mental Health in New Zealand*, vol. 3, no 1. (November 1986) pp. 50–63.

Afro-Caribbean Mental Health Association, 35–37 Electric Avenue, Brixton, London SW9 8JP.

Jerome Agel, *Rough Times* (Ballantine, 1973).

Association of Community Health Councils, *Annual Report* (1989).

Ingrid Barker and Edward Peck (eds), *Power in Strange Places* (Good Practices in Mental Health, 1987).

Barclay Report *Social Workers – Their Roles and Tasks* (Bedford Square Press, 1982).

Virginia Beardshaw, 'Conscientious Objectors at Work', *Social Audit* 1981.

Lynne Berry and Brian Jones *Whose Social Services?* (Association of Metropolitan Authorities, 1988).

Anny Brackx and Catherine Grimshaw (eds), *Mental Health Care in Crisis* (Pluto Press, 1989).

David Brindle, 'Nurse Suspended After Complaining', *The Guardian* (15 Aug. 1990).

Phil Brown (a), *The Transfer of Care: Psychiatric Deinstitutionalisation and its Aftermath* (Routledge & Kegan Paul, 1985).

Phil Brown (b) (ed.), *Mental Health Care and Social Policy* (Routledge, 1985) p. 207.

CMH, *Learning About Self Advocacy, Booklet 1: What is Self Advocacy?* (1988).

Peter Campbell, 'Giants and Goblins', in Edward Barker and Ingrid Pecks, *Power in Strange Places: User Empowerment in Mental Health Services* (Good Practices in Mental Health, 1987).

David Carson, 'Coded Messages on a Matter of Principle', *The Health Service Journal* (18 January 1990).

Judy Chamberlin, *On our Own* (MIND, 1988).

Deborah Cooper and John Hersov, *We Can Change the Future – Self Advocacy for People with Learning Difficulties: A Staff Training Resource* (National Bureau for Handicapped Students, 1986).

Jocelyn Cornwell and Pat Gordon (eds), *An Experiment in Advocacy* (King's Fund, 1984).

Department of Health, 'Mental Health Act, 1983 – Code of Practice', HMSO 1990

Good Practices in Mental Health (GPMH), *Advocacy Information Pack – Advice and Advocacy Services for People with Psychiatric Disabilities* (1986).

Larry Gostin, 'What you in for Boy?', *MIND OUT*, June 1975a.

Larry Gostin, 'A Human Condition', *MIND*, 1975b.

J. Haffkens, G. Nijhof and E. Van Der Poel, 'Mental Health Care and the Opposition Movement in the Netherlands', *Social Science Medical*, vol. 22, no. 2 (1986) pp. 185–92.

Chris Halford, 'Changing Practices in Mental Health', *Voluntary Voice*, Oct. 1989.

Brian Harris, *The Islington Mental Health Forum – A Case Study in How to Get Users Involved* (GPMH, Jan. 1989).

John Harris, 'Citizen Advocacy: Four Lessons from the North American Experience', *Social Work Today* (6 April 1987).

Simon Hebditch, *Advocacy in Britain in Professionals and Volunteers – Partners or Rivals?*, Pat Gordon (ed.) (King's Fund, 1982).

Cherrill Hicks, 'How to Betray a Profession', *The Guardian* (16 July 1986).

Insight, 'Users' Charter', Brighton (January 1990).

Knud Jensen and Bent Pedersen (eds), *Commitment and Civil Rights of the Mentally Ill*, Proceedings of the conference in Copenhagen 12–15 August 1984, organised by SIND (the Danish National Society for the Mentally Ill) in collaboration with the World Federation for Mental Health (Copenhagen, 1985).

A. H. Katz and E. I. Bender, *The Strength in Us: Self-Help Groups in the Modern World* (Franklin Watts, 1976).

King's Fund, *Report on Mental Illness and Mental Deficiency Hospitals* (1955).

King's Fund Project Paper, 'The Advice and Representation Project at Springfield Hospital, 1982–1985', Number 59 (1986).

Mental Patients Union, 'The Need for a Mental Patients Union', unpublished paper (1972).

Neal Milner, 'The Symbols and Meanings of Advocacy', *International Journal of Psychiatry and Law, 1985.*

Colin Murray Advocacy Project, Bellsdyke Hospital, Larbert near Stirling, personal communication, 10 April 1990.

National Citizen Advocacy, *Citizen Advocacy: A Powerful Partnership* (NCA, 1988).

North West Consumer Network, *Consumer Network News*, no. 4, (January 1990).

Nottingham Advocacy Group, *Annual Report 1988–89* (NAG, Kilbourn Street, Nottingham NG3 1BQ).

Yvonne Pearson, 'A Plea for Asylum', SANE newsletter (Spring 1990).

Tom Rathwell, 'Stand up for Patient Rights', *The Health Service Journal* (18 January 1990).

Jim Read, 'Survivors of the Mental Health System Stand Up For Their Rights', *i to i* (December 1989–January 1990).

Judy Renshaw:, 'Consumers as Colleagues', *Community Care* (27 April 1989).

Resettlement Support Group, The Patients Association, North Manchester General Hospital (Psychiatry).

Stephen Rose and Bruce Black, *Advocacy and Empowerment – Mental Health: Care in the Community* (Routledge & Kegan Paul, 1985).

Bob Sang and John O'Brien, *Advocacy – the U.K. and American Experiences* (King's Fund, 1984).

Peter Sedgwick, *Psycho Politics* (Pluto, 1982).

Max Siporin, *Introduction to Social Work Practice* (Collier Macmillan, 1975).

Helen Smith, *Collaboration for Change* (King's Fund, January 1988).

Survivors Speak Out, *Self-Advocacy Action Pack – Empowering Mental Health Service Users* (SSO, 1988).

Jan Wallcraft, 'Winning Through against Fear and Contempt', *Community Care* (27 April 1989).

Irene Whitehill, *Report: Newcastle Advocacies Project – August 1988–October 1989* (NAP, February 1990).

Denise Winn, 'Human Network Halts the Spiral of Despair', *Independent* (28 Feb 1989).

8

Democracy in Strange Places

This chapter focuses on attempts to democratise mental illness services and on users running their own services. It looks at influences from Maxwell Jones and the 'therapeutic community' and some Italian, United States and Dutch developments. It concludes by examining the Canadian service brokerage system and relating it to mental illness.

Despite the valiant work of MIND and other campaigning groups, the struggle for full citizenship for psychiatric patients is far from accomplished. Not only do most patients have little influence on their services but they are also deprived of many democratic rights inside mental hospitals.

The fundamental right of adult citizens is to vote. Few long-stay psychiatric in-patients presently qualify. They may vote only if they meet certain conditions, which others, already living in the community – with or without a mental illness – do not have to comply with. The Representation of the People Act 1983 requires mental hospital residents to complete a special form, a 'Patient's Declaration', which requires details of name, age, address of hospital where they live and the address of the place where they would be living if they were not in hospital, or any address in the United Kingdom (other than a mental hospital) where they were resident in the past. This is the address for their registration to vote.

In 1984, only 319 patients (6.3 per cent) of a total mental hospital population in the North West of England of 6,195, completed these forms, and one whole hospital population (including residential staff!) was disenfranchised. By 1989, the position had improved slightly: 7.6 per cent of the total mental hospital population had completed registration forms and again one whole hospital population was disenfranchised.

There is a substantial difference between rhetoric and reality. The Minister's statement (Hansard, 1987) that the 1983 Act ensured that informal patients in mental hospitals are able to register as electors is unconvincing (Dyer, 1989). The struggle for democratisation of services, to gain users more power and influence, takes place against a backcloth of disenfranchisement.

Democracy on psychiatric hospital wards is minimal. A WHO report states: 'For hospitalized patients the ward is their daily environment. Yet the influence of patients on the rules in this environment remains small. Institutional rules and bureaucratic procedures often lead to situations in which the individual cannot develop and ultimately becomes alienated . . . the patient is expected to adapt to the needs of the institution rather than the other way round' (WHO, 1989).

There have been a number of experiments in encouraging patients to play more influential roles in running psychiatric services. Some were inspired by Maxwell Jones's notions of 'therapeutic community' which were extremely influential in the 1960s and 1970s but have waned considerably, as we saw in Chapter 3, 'Winds and Tides'. Jones describes the elements of this approach:

> what distinguishes a therapeutic community from other comparable treatment centres is the way in which the institution's total resources, staff, patients, and their relatives, are self-consciously pooled in furthering treatment. This implies, above all, a change in the usual status of patients. In collaboration with the staff, they now become active participants in their own therapy and that of other patients and in many aspects of the unit's general activities. This is in marked contrast to their relatively more passive, recipient role in conventional regimes. (Jones, 1968, pp. 85–6)

What happens when democratisation approaches of this kind go badly wrong is conveyed by Claire Barron (1988). She describes radical innovation in a psychiatric day hospital in the 1970s which involved using psycho-analysis in a large group setting. This relied heavily on the charismatic figure of the Medical Director. She writes of the daily groups: 'but until the medical director arrived, there would be an air of expectancy as before a theatrical performance. Without this charismatic figure all was dead and mundane. With him the strange and wonderful game had meaning: the desire for self-discovery, the acceptance of the darker side of our natures, the mystery tour whose destination was unnamed and unknown.'

The central idea was that 'it was their [the users'] hospital to run and control as they chose'. After about a year, however, the dream of therapy for everyone in a ruleless setting began to falter:

The revelation the patients had been waiting for seemed as far off as ever. The day hospital therapy no longer appeared to be the perfect solution to mental illness. Little by little, the family became less at one with itself. Whereas previously the patients accepted that everything they said and did, be it drinking or their intervention in a group session, was unconsciously motivated, gradually some of them began to resist the relentless psycho-analytic gaze.

. . . Their belief that they had a right, even a duty, to participate in decision making in the community waned as they started to feel their contributions were constantly being neutralised by interpretations based on sexualised or murderous fantasies. The democratic ideology began to wear a little thin, too, with the gradual realisation that behaviour was being controlled by means of the therapy itself. But still they could not doubt their leader. He still held sway in the group.

Gradually, as the discord increased, the medical director became more extreme. Every single action and thought was now deemed to be evidence of pathology . . . Practical needs remained unmet. The day hospital became filthy without a cleaner and the patients had to go to their GPs for their medical certificates . . . Eventually, the conflict between the patient's own perceptions and the view maintained by the staff was brought to an abrupt end. One Friday before Christmas the staff uncharacteristically pinned up a letter on the wall of the large group room, announcing that from the New Year all free lunches and fare reimbursements would end. The patients seized on this action as evidence of the repression they had sensed but which had been denied for so long . . .

Despite its radical image the day hospital exemplified the process by which, through a regime of therapy, the progress of patients was defined by staff in terms of psychiatric health or illness, progress and regression. Therapy in these terms can be seen as a kind of 'degradation therapy' whereby the patient has to take on the staff's version of himself as a condition of treatment: namely that his actions, attitudes and statements are governed solely by his pathology. (Barron, 1988)

This is a sensitive description of the entangled themes of therapy and democratisation. Giving power with strings attached means it can be taken back when the giver is displeased. Maxwell Jones and others were the heirs of the 'moral management' tradition of the early nineteenth century. Like the Tukes in the eighteenth and early nineteenth centuries, Jones was concerned with the good of people rather than the transfer of power.

A recent MIND–Richmond Fellowship study team report continues that tangled web:

No person has an inalienable right to be involved in every decision about their lives. However, service users merit the right to be involved in decisions which affect them directly as part of the recognition of their individual worth and individual dignity. It must be recognised however that users' aims and needs and staff aims are not necessarily compatible. Short-term external quality of life outcomes connected with comfort and safety may not always be compatible with long-term therapeutic aims. User involvement should be set against a background of therapeutic reality and within the context of maximising individual human and civil rights.

Phrases like 'therapeutic reality' are both vague and dangerous. They conceal authoritarianism. Words like 'merit' imply that rights have to be earned and deserved (MIND–Richmond Fellowship, 1990).

In contrast, Chamberlin argues for genuine democracy. She sees the first obstacle as 'mental patients are taught to think of their differences as "symptoms" which require professional expertise to treat'. She describes the alternative as: 'providing help with needs as defined by clients; voluntary participation; clients to choose involvement in some aspects of services without being required to participate in others; help comes from anyone and everyone; overall direction is in the hands of service recipients; responsibility of the service is to the client' (Chamberlin, 1988, p. 329). This model moves away from the cartwheel systems implicit in Barron's account, where staff are automatically central to the communication system.

Some British mental illness services have begun to be strongly influenced by Dutch developments. In 1970, a unique committee of residents was formed in a large psychiatric hospital concerned with leisure and amenities. By 1975, the first national meeting of eight resident's councils (*Patientenraad*) plus representatives from four other hospitals, took place. Two years later, there were 35 councils in the 41 psychiatric hospitals in Holland.

The councils differ a great deal in composition. Some work co-operatively with hospital managers whilst others meet hostility. The advantage of regular national meetings was that the best councils served as models for the rest. After the initial dynamic period, stagnation followed. Meetings got bogged down in often trivial discussions about leisure and food. A national organisation was developed in 1980 to create a legal framework for all the residents' councils. A government report suggesting general guidelines and tasks for the councils was accepted unanimously.

Each hospital ward is eligible to send a representative, although few of the longer-stay and psycho-geriatric units are able. Management is required to give councils notification about relevant planning issues. I attended a residents' council at Veldwijk where a lively meeting (March 1988) discussed the ethics of a new research proposal. This council received some secretarial help from the hospital. It was interesting that almost all the issues were of a general nature with few individual complaints.

The Veldwijk Patients Council is based on a contract drawn up between the Council and the General Director of the hospital (Veldwijk, 1985): 'The patients council aims at the promotion of collective interests and the vindication of the rights of patients admitted to Veldwijk and at a better legal status for admitted psychiatric patients in general.'

The patients' council is asked for advice by the board of directors before decisions are taken about:

(a) changes in policy regarding the legal position of admitted patients;
(b) changes in the delivery of treatment by the hospital;
(c) changes in the character of a ward;
(d) enlargement or shrinking of the size of the hospital;
(e) all other planned policies that directly regard the interests of patients.

There has been a tendency for patients' advocates to syphon off most of the individual patients' complaints, some of which had formerly found their way through the council network. Patients' advocates usually sit on the council to lubricate co-operation (Abbott, 1986).

There is now a national office in Utrecht providing support through part-time development workers. Currently, there are 43 councils in 45 institutions. Patients' councils are gradually being developed in the addiction units and some community based services, although this is a slow business.

In Veldwijk Hospital there is also a 'family council' (Hardeman, 1987). The long-stay patients are usually not fully represented through the patient's councils. In 1978 a couple of relatives decided to form a council to further the interests of long-stay patients. In 1981 there was an agreement drawn up between the family council and the General Director.

The family council meets monthly. Relatives tend to take an interest in other patients who have no relatives. Over the years the council has criticised the lack of quality dental care; discussed incontinence; clearer accountability for patients' monies; made points about the side-effects of major tranquillisers like tardive dyskenesia. There is a system now on long-stay wards where the family of the patients, with his or her consent, receives an annual report about his condition and the medication prescribed.

In my discussion with the Chairperson at Veldwijk family council, natural tensions became explicit. Relatives and patients' interests are not necessarily the same or even similar. For example, relatives may have a vested interest in the patients staying within the hospital and not moving back into the community. Whilst family councils can represent people who are too profoundly handicapped to find a role in Patients' Councils or seek the help of an advocate, citizen advocacy – one-to-one volunteers, representing people not able to speak for themselves – is largely unknown.

What has all this participation really accomplished? It has improved the general quality of services but are there more gains than that? Dutch psychiatry seems to be more socially concerned, aware of the influence of both poverty and loneliness on mental illness. But Van de Graaf suggests that userist systems may lead merely to cosmetic changes: 'People now call for small-scale facilities in the neighbourhood. This is very valid, but if the nature of the services doesn't change, then I'm really afraid it will be more of the same wine but in new barrels. It would lead to more social control, this time almost ratified by advocacy and user organisations' (Abbott, 1986).

Planning mental illness services is complex. There are fundamental and irreconcilable disagreements between users and professionals about the nature of mental illness. In the planning bodies, at best, there are one or two users amongst twenty people. This can be mere tokenism. 'Clients are not taken seriously by psychiatry. Their wishes and aspirations are seen as syndromes, clinical pictures, personality disorders' (Wiegant, 1988).

Patients' associations battle for a radical reappraisal of the way their members are treated, often seen as the sinister by-product of a hostile capitalist society. They attempt to make an intolerable system more humane, ironically perhaps even extending its shelf-life. They are split between making systems more tolerable for existing users and at the same time working towards structures which can replace them. It is easy to get sucked into sustaining an isolated psychiatric resource when the need is for a demedicalised stress centre just round the corner.

Nottingham developments were directly influenced by the Dutch experience. Barker and Peck, then based in that city, had visited Holland. The first development worker for Nottingham Patients' Council was the Dutchman and former psychiatric patient, Wouter Van de Graaf. Nottingham Patients Council Support Group (NPCSG) a mixed group of users and former users, got involved in training staff in user awareness, both locally and nationally. They formed patients-only groups on wards as well as patients' councils on the Dutch model (NPCSG, 1988). There were historical precedents for patients and staff working closely together. In 1922, in what the *Nottingham Journal* called the 'most sensational strike of modern time', staff at Radcliffe Asylum barricaded themselves in the wards in an attempt to prevent their 60-hour week being extended. When police and bailiffs came in force to evict them, lunatics fought side by side with staff to repel the invaders 'in scenes of the wildest description' (Lowe, 1988).

The NPCSG began rather more sedately in 1986. After De Graaf's development work, there was no paid worker. Volunteers, mainly with a psychiatric consumer background and helped by Nottingham MIND, visited wards in Mapperley psychiatric hospital, where there was a small and remote office and in the District General Hospital psychiatric unit. 'The small scheme quickly had a substantial national impact. There was widespread interest and the 6 to 12 volunteers got tired and morale was low. Without paid support, there were difficulties within the group. People moved on, lost interest or got jobs. Newcomers could perceive the group as a clique. At the Dale psychiatric day centre, run by Nottingham social services department, the achievements have been marked. Users have been involved in discussions on policy. On the Mapperley hospital wards the progress has been slow. The degree of sympathy with user involvement is variable – from very sympathetic to outright hostile . . . The group was thrown off one ward for a while and denied access to others. The Mental Illness Unit could withdraw recognition and turn off its funds. But if the group, because of these pressures, tamely accepts that user-involvement is just a token, will it not fall apart anyway?' (Davey, 1990).

There is general low morale among psychiatric staff who feel badly treated which has a knock-on effect on patients. Users' involvement is understood as something which is tagged on rather than as a whole new philosophy . . . It needs to be very clear that the support group is not a Patients Council. Issues must rise from patients' concerns not from those of the Support Group. But patients will need help in clarifying their complaints and in developing strategies for seeing that something is done about them. (Davey, 1988)

Progress was speedier in the psychiatric unit of the Queens Medical Centre in Nottingham. Regular patients-only meetings are held. Minutes of the various meetings (Davey, 1990) cover catering problems (cups and metal cutlery continued to go missing); information on medication; need for more activities to stave off boredom. A member of the Council Support Group follows up issues with the relevant staff.

Patients' councils are spreading rapidly in England and Wales. Of the nine large mental hospitals in Wales, four have active councils – Whitchurch, Cardiff; Glanrhyd, mid-Glamorgan; Parc, mid-Glamorgan; and Mid-Wales, Powys (MIND in Wales, 1990). The enthusiasm is immense but the real question remains as to how cosmetic they are.

No one could describe the work of the Italian, Franco Basaglia, as cosmetic. He argued robustly for the politicisation of mental illness:

The automatic way in which, in the asylum, the diagnosis of illness means the prognosis of its chronic nature, followed in turn by permanent confinement, has, for more than a century, insured control over inclusion in or exclusion from the labour market of those social classes which have been isolated and relegated to the margins of the productive organisation . . . In Italy the situation has been characterised by further polarization: experiments of alternative management of the institutions have been able to exploit the new directives to render the asylum obsolete and to plan an alternative system of services, whereas the majority of psychiatric hospitals continue to be based on the concept of asylum as a prison-like institution cut off from its surroundings. (Basaglia, 1980)

The professional movement formed around these ideas was called Psichiatria Democratica. Their major breakthrough came in Trieste (Bennett, 1985). San Giovanni, the old mental hospital, now houses the administration of the psychiatric services, a community mental health centre and co-operatives, the Arts Centre and a number of flats for ex-patients. The main services operate through seven community psychiatric centres which have beds in different parts of the city and district. The relationships between staff and patients, who are called 'users', are warm and friendly. There are few obvious distinctions. Everybody is on first-name terms. Some observers (Jones and Poletti, 1986) suggest that the original asylum is still open but more hidden and dispersed. The hospital still houses 200 patients who could not find outside accommodation but they do not live in an institutional environment. There are more patients in an alcoholic unit; in the university clinic; in a hostel linked with the drug clinic; accommodated in the different centres; and there are patients in the lodging houses as well as in the *convenzionati* – private nursing homes.

Two lines for psychiatric reform existed in Italy: 'de-hospitalisation', the rundown and eventual closure of psychiatric institutions; and 'de-institutionalisation', the radical review of congregated systems of service provision. The passing of law 180 in 1978 put an emphasis on the treatment of patients in community based services. Article 6 states, 'From the coming into force of this law, mental health treatments which require hospitalization and which are at the expense of the State or public bodies and institutions are carried out in the mental care centers.'

Despite law 180, the conflict between de-hospitalisation and de-institutionalisation continues:

> In one case, the transformation of psychiatry has resulted in its users achieving some form of organised, public expression and a certain level of autonomy in managing their own problems. In the other case, calls from family associations (which have been formed to request new kinds of internment) sometimes accompany the silence, isolation and impotence of the users . . . The groups lobbying for a return to internment are proposing and requesting more than just a few 'protected' institutions. They want to see a return to the principle of authority – of the family and of science – where the weak are invalidated by professional custody, the reasons for suffering are stifled and the 'cure' is considered achieved only when the patient returns to 'normality'. For their part, user associations do not opt merely for space and regulation within the services or with regard to psychiatry. They are organised against the future of social invisibility which was built in the past for them by the walls of psychiatric hospitals. (Giannichedda, 1989)

Giannichedda also notes:

the work co-operatives based on one created in Trieste by a small group of about 30 psychiatric patients who undertook hospital cleaning and gardening work. Under the old institutional system, this had been called occupational therapy. Within the co-operative it became work which was paid for by the local administration. There are currently 65 co-operatives of this type in Italy with about 2,000 associates. They have been aligned into the National Co-ordinating Body for Co-operatives against Marginalization. (ibid)

A more sardonic report questions real progress in Italy.

There is a gradual decrease in the number of persons cared for in public and private psychiatric hospitals (especially in public ones), although mortality tends to become an increasingly important factor in this trend . . . The quality of care extended to those who remain in hospital falls below an acceptable level, although there has been no decrease in the ratio between in-patients and practitioners. Even though it is explicitly prohibited by law, many psychiatric hospitals still agree to admit both discharged in-patients and those never previously admitted. This makes it unlikely that the use of those services for psychiatric purposes will be abandoned in the near future.

Albeit slowly, the decrease in the numbers of in-patients in mental hospitals is accompanied by a numerical increase in district and out-patient services. However, the quality of care provided and the regional distribution of services are not acceptable. The reorganisation has benefited hospital and out-patient services, but community care facilities remain inadequate. (Crepet, 1990)

Contrast that with an account from Franca Basaglia, the wife of the late Franco:

One characteristic of the Italian movement has been the focusing on the transformation of mental hospitals into places where the needs of patients are discovered instead of these patients being repressed and hidden by a culture which does not understand their disorder and regards it as incurable. Hospitals were transformed into places where a new way of dealing with psychic disorders could emerge which would tackle the practical and global nature of factors constituting the suffering they caused. The struggle therefore was aimed specifically at the mental institution and its inevitable violence and also at the scientific ideology which has become dogmatic and reinforced the incomprehensible nature of the disorder, and hence the 'diversity' of the sufferer. (Basaglia, 1989)

An important British attempt to democratise mental illness services is at Tontine Road in Chesterfield (Milroy and Hennelly, 1989). Run by Derbyshire Social Services department, it was originally a traditional day centre housing a wide range of activities.

Power and powerlessness are central experiences for everyone in the provision or use of mental health services. For those of us with the responsibility to provide services, the exercise of professional discretion and judgement involves the use of power over fellow citizens who turn to us for help. People using mental health services lose, forfeit or actively seek to dispose of power and control over their own lives. The character of modern professional health and social services in such that loss of power is inevitably encouraged. Our society has generated strong images of omni-competent professionals who soothe, cure and remove the hurt, pain and problems of living . . .
  Tontine Rd centre, which provides a base for the North Derbyshire Mental Health Services Project, is used by over 33 community groups and services. The organisation and operation of the centre is focussed through a Management Committee made up of representatives of all groups using the facility . . . The social support groups we have developed which provide a focus for the work of the project, are all formally constituted self-regulating independent community groups. Project workers and other colleagues have to accept specific responsibility to provide material advice and support. The constitution of these groups established a form of 'Service Charter' setting out the rights and duties of those providing the service as well as those using it . . . A charter challenges the ultimate power of profes-

sionalism – the power to make and alter rules, manipulate procedures, and maintain control. (Milroy and Hennelly, 1989)

In the United States, patient-run alternatives are reasonably common and many receive public funding. The Oakland Independence Support Centre in California was started by a mental health clients' network to meet some problems of homelessness, from which many had suffered. It was seen as essential to understand users' needs, to supply encouraging role models and to attract people who mistrusted the professional services. The centre provides a social centre; a place to eat; to get a bath; store valuables; a mailing address; a source of help with welfare benefits and finding housing and jobs; a place where it is safe to express distress. At any one time, it helps around 250 people, with 100 callers each day:

> There is a strong emphasis on democratic participation by users. They comprise more than half the Board which oversees the ex-user staff. Centre users make all the rules. These tend to be strictly enforced – no drink or drugs on the premises, users' weapons stored with the Centre staff, no racist language. Psychiatry is kept at a distance . . . It is local businessmen and community leaders who join the Centre's users on its Board, not a single mental health professional. (Patmore, 1988)

The Vancouver Mental Patients' Association (MPA) in British Columbia, Canada was created in 1971 by a group of ex-psychiatric patients who felt that the mental health system did not address their needs. They concentrated on decent reasonably priced housing. MPA's first houses in 1973 were rented and run collectively by people who initially met through a drop-in centre. Since then they have purchased a variety of other housing stock, including apartment buildings.

Another way forward for Canadians has been through co-operatives. Abel Enterprises (Haldimand-Norfolk Work Group) of Simcoe, Ontario was formed to create employment and provide vocational training for Simcoe community residents who experience short-term and long-term mental health problems. Most workers are diagnosed as schizophrenic. Abel Enterprises is a business which takes on a variety of contracts for skilled and unskilled labour. It provides a place to work, a regular hourly wage and the opportunity for members to express their ideas and talents in a realistic way. It has 'no coddling' philosophy (Church and Revell, 1990).

That kind of self-help movement has considerable implications for democratisation. People with direct experience of psychiatry and their families are setting up and running their own services:

> The self-help groups which have arisen among different categories of the ill, disabled and otherwise medically eligible (for example pregnant women) may have originated as a response to failures in provision from the public health service; but the ideals that they subserve, namely in monitoring and control of the individual's own health destiny by himself or herself, form completely valid objectives in their own right. (Sedgwick, 1982, p. 195)

Kanis describes the development of self-help groups for families who have a member with manic-depression (MD) in Scotland: 'Most groups revolve round an exchange of experiences in a number of different subjects, e.g. medicines, especially librium and its monitoring; brushes with the police; forcible treatment; discussion on employment and whether it is sensible to tell the employers that one is manic-depressive; insurance declarations; travel in the USA and problems in obtaining a visa.' The MD groups also provide special support. They discuss 'the guilt families feel about the cause of the illness; fight discrimination . . . Mania can be a purgative of friends and spouses.' 'Professional involvement has to be jealously limited to avoid eroding the concept of self-help' (Kanis, 1987).

'The Islington Women and Mental Health project grew out of a group of local women who found existing mental health services inadequate, and came together to support each other.' The group applied for funding and received a grant for the salary of one worker and office expenses in 1983.

> We see our role as enabling women to come together to share their pain and to make the connection between the pain and their external oppression. We hold a weekly drop-in every Tuesday. It operates on a discussion level and most women

come on an irregular basis, although a few attend weekly . . . it is somewhere to discuss problems and gain information in a safe environment with women who acknowledge that everybody has emotional problems. (Women in MIND, 1986)

A Canadian system with implications for mental illness services is service brokerage. It was developed not by professionals but by parents of mainly profoundly handicapped children in the Woodlands School (a large mental handicap hospital) near Vancouver in the mid-1970s, calling themselves the Woodlands Parents Group (WPG) (Brandon and Towe, 1989).

I met some WPG families when I visited Canada, and they shared their experiences. Like their British counterparts, they struggled with inequalities built into the existing social service systems. Through the inadequacy of community supports, mothers came close to emotional breakdown and the only option was to send their disabled offspring into Woodlands. The institutions took over control of their children. Parents tried to pretend that their children were better off, but in reality they were neglected in huge and grim institutions, with staff who were excessively defensive. Collectively, these parents realised that their increasing anger and outrage was a legitimate reaction to the individual powerlessness that each experienced in struggling for the needs of their sons or daughters.

Initially, WPG developed strategies aimed at reforming the institution. They invented advocacy systems and programmes of regular 'case reviews' and quality evaluation whilst the institution tried to co-opt them like other parent pressure groups. The WPG soon recognised that if their children were to gain real power they must live as full participants within the community with all of the rights – social, economic and political – that entailed. They had to turn their back on traditional forms of systems ownership. When formal systems took over they split disabled individuals away from their family and friends and owned their 'clients'. Usually the most effective forms of advocacy, 'quality control', sources of love and affection – family and friends – were increasingly alienated.

Instead of allocating large sums of money directly to professionals and formal service systems, they envisioned funds allocated to the individual needs of each person with disabilities. This money would be used flexibly and dynamically to support him or her in a valued life within a neighbourhood. They had discovered *individualised funding.*

Individualised funding is the allocation of cash or credits to people on the basis of individual needs and strengths. This means money based on a plan submitted to the funding body that articulates the needs and requirements of an individual with disabilities. This can involve direct funding or some credit arrangements. Until now, funding arrangements have been heavily weighted towards block services and client groups, like hostels and adult training centres, rather than towards individuals. Block funding encourages block treatment and the growth of the primary importance of client groupings like 'mental illness' and 'mental handicap'. A funding agency allocates a sum of money towards leisure, occupational or accommodation support provided to a given number of people. Whether that money helps those assembled individuals becomes a secondary issue.

WPG also saw that even if parents and people with disabilities received money and resources, they might not have easy access to information and negotiation skills. They invented a professional, employed by an independent Board, who would plan on request under the control of the user and/or his family/friends. They had discovered *service brokerage.*

Service brokerage is community based and consumer controlled. Service brokers are employed by an independent Brokerage Board which provides the services and holds individual brokers accountable. The Board is a 'fixed point of response' providing technical services. The broker has no authority to make any decisions. His main function is to assist in the planning of services. He gathers information and synthesises it, keeping the client informed at each stage. His purpose is not to 'plan for' people who have a handicap and require community services but to assume that the individual can plan for his or her own life, but requires some support service to do this effectively. Consequently a brokerage service is offered on demand to the person who has the handicap. *Brokerage is simply an optional service for those with individualised funding or currently seeking it.* The broker may be asked to do many things or just one.

A fundamental problem is that knowledge about alternatives to formal systems of care and support is limited. It is difficult to get relevant information to make informed decisions. No single agency provides complete and accurate information about the location, cost, accessibility and quality of existing service option. People seeking alternatives stumble down endless tunnels. Brokerage forges links between purchasers of services and potential providers.

The broker acts like a travel agent. Some people may arrange their own holidays without the help of the travel agent. Others may use the travel agent, or the service broker, at their discretion, if they want help with one or a number of different information gathering or planning tasks. Some people may want a lot of assistance; others will manage by themselves. People want to purchase services, so he provides information about possible sources. *The service broker negotiates continuous individualised service agreements which assist living independently.* All plans must be agreed with the individual and her/his family and/or friends.

In 1976, WPG met with the Minister of Human Resources (British Columbia) to propose an alternative to institutional living for their children. The Minister agreed to divert some funding which would have gone to the hospital. In 1978, the parents established a not-for-profit organisation called the 'Community Living Society'. The first ten children left Woodlands Hospital to live in the community in the same year.

The idea soon got lost in a fug of empire building and provincial government pressures. The essence was that the individual with disabilities would receive the cash (or its equivalent) to cover costs involved in being disabled. If and when that person needed help it would ordinarily come from family and friends. The more severe the degree of multiple and profound disabilities, the greater the role of family and friends in making informed and responsible decisions on behalf of the person. The basic assumption was that given the opportunity, family/friends could be effective advocates, although there would be some clashes of interest. State funding would help cement close relationships rather than, as so often in the past, helping to erode them.

In Alberta they have provided individual financial packages for a number of people labelled 'mentally ill'. With their broker from the Calgary Association for Independent Living (CAIL), Heather MacLean, I visited Vance and Gerry who share an apartment in Calgary. Vance is twenty years old. He met Gerry when visiting CAIL for help.

'I was in institutions for years. The last one an institution for about two hundred kids – a mixture of different young people and children. People were drugged up to the eyes. I was on stelazine. It was boring and there wasn't much freedom and lots of punishment. We were locked in rooms for hours if we misbehaved. The food was terrible. There was a ten foot high fence around the whole place.

It's a big improvement here. We've lived in the present flat for about five months. I do most of the cooking and Gerry most of the washing. We have our quarrels but we get along pretty fine. I am trying to get a job but with my record, work is hard to find. I have an interview next week for a janitor's position. I spend my days working on the computer – various games and reading science fiction books, particularly by Arthur C. Clarke.'

Gerry is thirty-six years old and originally came from Quebec. He showed me his fine collection of tropical fish and less attractive assortment of prize mice. He spent many years in the Albertan state mental institution. He has had no contact with his family for many years. On discharge, he went to Calgary, made contact with CAIL and gradually came off modecate. He got a flat and through the broker he applied for individualised funding. He received enough money to pay for a support worker. With Heather MacLean's help, he interviewed twenty-two applicants before appointing Helen as his support worker. Her salary was paid through a financial trustee. 'I appointed her because she didn't look like a nurse. Helen helped me gain more independence. She taught me to cook and get more confidence.'

When Heather MacLean found Gerry, he was isolated and in hiding.

'He had no help in a dirty basement flat. He had become a recluse, constantly threatening suicide. We arranged for him to get money for staff support; helped him to develop friendships; and provided information about existing services which he could use. Now, he's doing really well. He has lots of friends including Vance. He works at an AutoWrecking Company. He's learning new skills in engineering.

Two and a half years ago, Gerry received 2200 dollars monthly because he needed extensive support. Now, Gerry gets

900 dollars a month because he's feeling much better. With that money he hires two personal support workers. They help with psychological and counselling support – budgeting, talking through any difficulties or decisions. They provide a schedule of hours during the week, drawn up in a contract. He can also phone them at any time.'

Democratisation is no easy option. It can easily conceal, as we saw in Barron's account, tarted-up colonialism. It not only needs attitudinal changes in professionals but the acquisition of new skills. Tyson describes an attempt to involve users in a traditional psychiatric day centre in making important decisions about the service:

The resistance from members was enormous. Our members are largely very institutionalised, routinised people – people used to strict regimes and the security these bring; most are in their forties and fifties. The staff group is younger, thirtyish, enthusiastic, some with social work training, all with a belief in enabling people to grow and develop.

There was a giant 'no' from the members. The attitude was that the staff should do it. We are a strong staff group, and we learnt quickly that the 'over to you folks' strategy cannot work. We know that we have to provide the structures, the bedrock of security which might enable user to take some control. We have to go at their pace, not ours. (Tyson, 1987)

Brotherton points out further dangers:

There is a great danger of 'tokenism' when users are represented on formal committees. Seats on such bodies do not necessarily mean any additional influence in decision-making. People at the seminar (Greater London Association of Community Health Councils) spoke of the difficulties in being a sole user in the company of experts . . . It is important that ways of including the user in decision-making are not imposed suddenly from above, but develop at a pace and in a style suited to the users themselves. (Brotherton, 1988)

References

Max Abbott, 'Patient and Ex-Patient Advocacy in the Netherlands: Interview with Wouter De Graaf', *Community Mental Health in New Zealand*, vol. 3, no. 1 (November 1986) pp. 50–66.

G. Back, *Zwangssterilisation in Nationalsozialism* (Westdeutscher Verlag, Oplanden, 1986).

Ingrid Barker, 'Powerful Remedies', *OPEN MIND* (19 December 1986).

Ingrid Barker and Edward Peck, *Power in Strange Places* (Good Practices in Mental Health, 1986).

Claire Barron, *From Asylum to Anarchy* (Free Association, 1988).

Franco Basaglia, 'Problems of Law and Psychiatry: The Italian Experience', *International Journal of Law and Psychiatry*, vol. 3, (1980) pp. 17–37.

Franca Basaglia, 'Italian Psychiatric Reform as a Reflection of Society', in Shulamit Ramon (ed.), *Psychiatry in Transition* (Routledge, 1989).

D. H. Bennett, 'The Changing Pattern of Mental Health Care in Trieste', *International Journal of Mental Health*, 14(1985) pp. 70–92.

David Brandon and Noel Towe, *Free to Choose* (Good Impressions, 1989).

Paul Brotherton, 'Putting Consumers First', *The Health and Social Services Journal* (14 July 1988).

Judy Chamberlin, *On Our Own* (MIND, 1988).

Kathryn Church and David Revell, 'User Involvement in Mental Health Services in Canada: A Work in Progress', in *Report of Common Concerns: International Conference on User Involvement in Mental Health Services* (MIND, 1990).

P. Crepet, 'A Transition Period in Psychiatric Care in Italy Ten Years After the Reform', *British Journal of Psychiatry*, vol. 156 (January 1990) pp. 27–36.

Brian Davey, 'Users' Councils in Nottingham', *Asylum* (Spring 1988).

Brian Davey, personal communication (February 1990).

Lindsay Dyer, 'Lost Citizens', *OPEN MIND*, no. 37 (February/March 1989).

Maria Grazia Giannichedda, 'Against a Future of Social Invisibility', in Shulamit Ramon (ed.), *Psychiatry in Transition* (Routledge, 1989).

Chris Halford, 'Changing Practices in Mental Health', *Voluntary Voice* , no. 39 (October 1989).

W. J. Hardeman, 'A Family Council in a Psychiatric Hospital', unpublished paper (27 October 1987).

Hansard, Mrs Edwina Currie (12 November 1987).

Knud Jensen and Bent Pedersen (eds) *Commitment and Civil Rights of the Mentally Ill*, Proceedings of the conference in Copenhagen 12–15 August 1984 organised by SIND (the Danish National Society for the Mentally Ill) in collaboration with the World Federation for Mental Health (Copenhagen, 1985).

Kathleen Jones and Alison Poletti, 'The "Italian Experience" Reconsidered', *British Journal of Psychiatry*, 148(1986) pp. 144–50.

Maxwell Jones, *Social Psychiatry in Practice* (Pelican, 1968).

Bernie Kanis, 'Seeds of Support for Scottish Manic Depressive Families', in Nancy Drucker (ed.), *Creating Community Mental Health Services in Scotland*, vol. 2 (Community Services in Practice, Scottish Association for Mental Health, 1987).

Andy Lowe, 'Patients Groups Change Mental Health Service', *Social Work Today* (4 August 1988).

Andrew Milroy and Rick Hennelly, 'Changing Our Professional Ways', in *Mental Health Care in Crisis*, edited by Anny Brackx and Catherine Grimshaw (Pluto, 1989).

MIND in Wales, personal communication (February 1990).

MIND–Richmond Fellowship study team report, *Quality in Community Mental Health Care* (January 1990).

Nottingham Patients Council Support Group – Information Pack, 114 Mansfield Road, Nottingham (1988).

Charles Patmore, 'Is Patient Power Coming to Britain?', *Community Psychiatry – Its Practice and Management*, no. 3 (November 1988).

Peter Sedgwick, *Psycho Politics* (Pluto, 1982) p. 195.

Helen Smith, *Collaboration for Change* (King's Fund, 1988).

Survivors Speak Out, 'A Charter of Needs and Demands', *New Directions* (March 1988).

Andrew Tyson, 'User Involvement: Going Beyond the Buzz-Words to a New Climate', *Social Work Today* (27 July 1987).

Veldwijk Psychiatric Hospital, Ermelo, Holland, Agreement of Co-operation Between the Board of Directors of Psychiatric Hospital Veldwijk and the Patients' Council of Veldwijk (1985).

Jan Wallcraft, 'Winning Through against Fear and Contempt', *Community Care* (27 April 1989).

Hans Wiegant, 'Users' Councils in Holland', *Asylum* (Spring 1988).

Denise Winn, 'Human Network Halts the Spiral of Despair', *Independent* (28 Feb. 1989).

Women in MIND, *Finding Our Own Solutions – Women's Experiences of Mental Health Care* (MIND, 1986).

World Health Organisation (WHO), *Consumer Involvement in Mental Health and Rehabilitation Services* (Division of Mental Health, 1989).

9

Innovation without Change?

What we are experiencing in mental illness services is the rhetoric of participation and userism rather than actual practice. It has become highly fashionable to be a 'consumerist'. As we have seen, that means vastly different things to different people. To most it simply means improvements in quality: 'consumer choice is another form of quality control . . . better information is a central aspect of this choice' (Secretary of State, 1989). To some it means the genuine extension of democratic processes – users appointing staff, managing budgets and, if desired, taking their individualised funding and designing their own services.

The good news is that many organisations already act on some of those principles. 'Just under a third of statutory departments and nearly half of a sample of voluntary organisations surveyed in England, Scotland and Wales already have written policies to involve service users.' Beresford and Croft argue that support and access are crucial to success in involvement. 'People need to be offered personal support and skills to take part, combined with suitable structures and opportunities for involvement in social services agencies.' Sardonically they ask 'Perhaps the key question now is will the massive changes that are taking place in social care herald greater user choice and say or be just another financial and administrative rejigging and shift of professional power? (Beresford and Croft, 1990).

This apparent progress on participation takes place against grim and graphic scenes, flashed around the world by international TV networks. Film from Romania and the island of Leros in Greece showed both mentally ill and mentally handicapped hospital patients ill-fed, naked and covered in excrement. Such scenes are the extremes of an ordinary continuum. 'In nearly every country people with a mental disorder suffer degrees of prejudice – often unnecessarily . . . it attracts stigma, fears and myths in many cultures . . . they face discrimination and treatment far worse than the rest of the population' (Heginbotham, 1987).

Internationally, psychiatric patients ordinarily forfeit basic human rights. They lose the right to vote in Japan and India. In Egypt, Holland and many other European countries, they lose the right to administer their own property. In Japan, Egypt and Israel they lose the right to receive uncensored mail. 'In most countries, if a patient threatened to sue his/her psychiatrist, it would be seen as final proof of madness' (Cohen, 1988).

In Britain, between four and five million people consult heir family doctors each year about depression and anxiety. More than 250,000 people have been diagnosed as having schizophrenia at some point in their lives. Up to 500,000 people have senile dementia and numbers increase as the population gets an older profile. We are seeing the rapid psychiaticisation of ordinary human life which conceals the overall deterioration in the quality of human relationships. Sadly, we are moving towards a society based on individual achievement and independence rather than interdependence, with all the loneliness and isolation which that inevitably brings.

Most long-term and chronically sick people are unemployed and live on social security. Large proportions are women and black, the categories most socially marginalised. They are treated by a system which is both sexist, inherently racist and still grossly stigmatising. Professionalised visions of 'mental health' are commonly aggressive and masculine as well as mono-cultural. So far, our participative systems have barely involved these people and those inequalities.

Most people are the walking symptoms of grave and increasing socio-economic problems. They have experienced years of chronic distress. Often they come from poor-quality environments, living in shoddy housing with few job opportunities and a constant struggle against poverty. My own adult experience of depression and treatment was the boomerang effect of years of poverty and incessant childhood battering at the fists and boots of my father in Sunderland.

Our mental illness service processes disproportionate numbers of poor, devalued and isolated people and mainly drugs them. 'Rather than having individually tailored treatment programmes everyone seems to get the same treatment – whatever their diagnosis. The majority of people had received most of the drugs in the psychiatric arsenal, quite often in combination prescriptions.' Nearly half of this sample of 500 mental illness patients had received ECT (MIND/Roehampton Institute, 1990).

Our existing systems prefer to pathologise or punish individuals rather than tackle deep-rooted social inequalities. We provide short-term hostels for beggars rather than proper homes with adequate incomes. Widespread changes in housing patterns, employment opportunities and fair social security policies are the winds and tides of just and reasonable mental illness policies. We need less policies motivated by psychiatric treatment and more inspired by ideas of what constitutes a healthy community (Brandon *et al.*, 1980). Although it may be highly commendable to wrestle swamp alligators and give first-aid to people falling from high cliffs, it may be more useful, if less exciting, to drain the swamps and put fences around the cliffs.

Mental illness professionals could be revolutionaries helping assign increased responsibility for problems to government and socio-economic structures rather than blaming distressed individuals. Currently professionals' training and attitudes are inherently conservative and self-serving. 'People of the same trade seldom meet together, even for merriment and diversion, but the conversation ends in a conspiracy against the public, or in some contrivance to raise prices' (Smith, 1776).

One danger is that professionals will increasingly squeeze out ordinary human involvement. Evidence from participation case studies in Hong Kong, Indonesia and The Philippines is extremely depressing. Health planners take a medical approach rather than a community development one because of their training. They make generalised and vague assumptions about the 'community'. Professional domination of services leads to the erosion of community participation. Health is not seen as a high priority for most people. It becomes the responsibility of doctors and nurses, the only people seen as capable of carrying out health activities (Rifkin, 1986).

Often patients and relatives see professionals as exclusively responsible for the helping process. They are seen as 'owning' it. Swedish research based on video recording, shows that the least disabled Alzheimer Syndrome patients help the most disabled patients with their meals when staff are not present. When psychiatric nurses join the group, the patients stop helping (Sandman, 1988).

> The prospects for increased participatory approaches in health arenas has to recognise not only the encouraging developments (e.g. the 'rights' legislation, global health program approaches, growth in community skills, freedom of information legislation, social action acceptability) but also the persistence of some long-standing impediments (e.g. entrenched medical dominance, antagonistic bureaucratic cultures, a centralist supremacy, an intractable political economy of health, inhibiting professional paradigms). (Brownlea, 1987)

Those are high and hostile mountains to climb.

WHO suggests a partnership in service management: 'the use of people with direct experience of mental health problems in assisting health professionals in prescribing and treatment development'. It reminds us more soberly that consultation 'can, however, be a way of marginalising those who are being consulted if their suggestions and advice are simply discarded'.

This involves an educational programme for health workers with four ingredients:

(a) the rationale for consumer involvement in the training of professional health workers;
(b) the importance of challenging stereotyped relationships of caregiver–receiver, competent–incompetent, etc.;
(c) the importance of giving credibility to the information and experiences of consumers imparted during such training;
(d) the importance of recognising the life-long negative implication of labels and diagnoses. (WHO, 1989)

Relatives and 'wounded healers' could act as important bridges to help services become more sensitive. Brian Davey of Nottingham MIND, a user himself, proposed training mental illness users as service providers (Davey, 1990). This means training the wounded healers, discussed earlier. The idea is that some former and current users get relevant training and eventually paid work. This parallels the Californian New Careers movement, popular in the 1970s (Briggs, 1972). Offenders trained as professionals in the penal and probation field. They met considerable resistances from other professionals.

The Swedes use 'peer counsellors'. Some disabled athletes who competed in the Olympic Games visit people in hospitals, mainly accident victims, and serve as role models. They feel that a person with a disability is helped to assimilate and overcome the condition much more quickly (van Dongen, 1990). This has implications for the mental illness field. We could train and support recovered mental illness patients in helping people still in hospital prepare for life outside. Professionals could work with recovered and recovering users in both group and individual work. This model is commonly used in both alcohol and drug rehabilitation.

We urgently need some 'separatist' projects. As in both Canada and the USA, Britain needs to see some investment going into services run exclusively by mental illness service users, especially in the fields of supported accommodation and employment. That would provide a very positive model and a challenge to some of the negative beliefs around people with psychiatric histories.

Changing professionals' attitudes and developing relevant skills will be difficult. Much of their destructiveness is unconscious and deeply embedded in almost unquestioned notions of the nature of professionalised interventions, much of which are highly masculine. Many of the structures which are supposed to support and nourish them, result in feeling even further devalued.

Ramon studied social workers concerned with the rundown and closure by 1993 of a large mental hospital in the south of England. All social workers welcomed the closure of the institution but none actively pursued user participation. they were marginalised and demoralised in a number of ways: marginalised within the local authority setting because mental illness work had low priority; marginalised within the hospital setting because the hospital general manager and consultant psychiatrists felt their work could be done by nurses. Demoralised professionals need systems and structures which appreciate their value and importance and foster both innovation and the acquisition of new skills (Ramon, 1990).

It is essential that users take more power and influence as well as being given it. The services can only radically improve and become more democratic on the backs of their increased expectations and feelings of power. 'How is freedom gained? It is taken: never given.

To be free, you must first assume your right to freedom' (Rushdie, 1990).

It is crucial that advocacy systems and patients' councils and other pressures towards democratisation flourish and expand:

> The determination of former users to organise is vital if anything is to change. This involves giving up what for many people is a very deep-rooted desire to find an expert with a magic answer and a magic pill to put them right, and taking power into their own hands instead. After all, if patients are no longer willing to play at being patients, psychiatric staff can no longer play at medical model psychiatry. (Johnstone, 1989)

Helen Smith outlines seven strategies: resourcing user groups; sharing information; changing working relationships; building partnerships; bringing in people who are severely disabled; training and support to change professional attitudes in particular; and challenging the prevailing ideology (Helen Smith, 1989).

Particularly important are groups which provide support for women and people from ethnic minorities. Dozens of small organisations struggle to develop self-help skills; run a drop-in centre; host a counselling phone-line. The well-women's centres, now established in many towns, often provide treatment, support and assistance. But for the most part they attract little funding and exist on the backs of a few admirable and energetic individuals who get increasingly exhausted.

Where the participation rhetoric is translated into positive islands of action, those services are often poorly funded and staffed. Here and there epic battles result in a patients' council; a self-advocacy group struggles; enlightened staff encourage users to have real power and influence. But, in the main, they have little real impact on the mainstream which greedily spends relatively vast resources – staff time and money.

The best known and oldest alternative is Geel in Belgium. The folk legend tells of the daughter of a heathen Irish prince, St Dympna, who fled from his incestuous passion to Geel early in the seventh century. He found her and slew both his daughter and her chaplain when she refused to return. Many alleviations of mental illness and epilepsy were attributed to her intercession and she became the patron saint of the insane (Attwater, 1965). From 1250 onwards 'lunatics' and 'mental defectives' were brought in increasingly large numbers to the town to seek cures. Nowadays 5 to 6 per cent of the town's population of 30,000 are mental illness patients coming from all over Belgium. Financial gain is just as important as altruism in this process. Such 'adult fostering' is regarded as a normal business but that does not account for the survival of this centuries-old tradition.

The 'boarders' in Geel prefer to stay with the host family. The system of family placement enjoys a well-developed supportive structure provided by the local psychiatric hospital (Sedgwick, 1982). Care-givers in Geel are not alone and isolated but part of an extensive caring system. Geelians have no fear of patients who, anyway, do not congregate in groups of 'their own kind'. This gives them the chance for a more healthy and integrated life (Roosens, 1979). Forty per cent of the patient-guests do regular shopping for their host families. There is some discrimination in the bars and cafes and other public places on grounds of mental status but often accompanied with joking banter.

As Geel has shown for more than seven centuries, our notions of 'community' or 'neighbourhood' are severely restricted. We do not understand community development strategies. We have simply used the idea of 'neighbourhood' in which to place a variety of statutory and voluntary institutions. Even so-called community services like hostels, psychiatric day centres and group homes are disguised institutions. They stand apart from the genuine community. Even energetic collaboration and partnerships between staff and mental illness patients cannot easily foster integration. It is difficult to integrate from segregated services (MacKnight, 1985). The mental illness industry employs more professionals to service the larger numbers of people defined as 'mentally ill', increasingly marginalising them.

Even real community-based options like those at Geel can be suffocated in bureaucracy. Our local Lancashire Social Services Department has a fifty-page document on the regulating of 'Adult Placements' – a kind of adult fostering (Lancashire Social Services, 1989). Unsurprisingly, with hundreds of conditions, few such placements are recruited.

In Holland, the numbers of foster families have declined where the number of sheltered homes, day centres, outpatient clinics and regional centres for mental illness patients have expanded:

Our personal observation is that psychiatric foster care is of great importance to society in general where there is a tendency to refer disturbed family members early to specialized mental health professionals and to withdraw family support. In such cases psychiatric foster families can have a mirror-function. They share their homes, televisions, newspapers and meals with the patients, but also times of happiness and grief. (Haveman and Maaskant, 1990)

As professionals increasingly take up a more central role in the provision of services, unpaid amateurs get pushed out to the edges. Relatives and other carers do the giant's slice of the work. Jordan comments: 'We should not see unpaid care and the sharing that takes place in families as unique. They are part of a much more extensive system of chosen and voluntary relationships in society, in which people organise themselves in small and large groups to get things done, to enjoy themselves, and to improve their quality of life' (DSS, 1989). This would involve a giant change in existing attitudes and services.

Jordan comments: 'Balancing the power of state officials by real freedom and choice for carers is part of the problem of creating public facilities and services which encourage active citizenship, participation and sharing, rather than restricting options and imposing passivity or constraint' (Jordan, 1990, p. 50). The influential House of Commons Social Services Select Committee suggested that carers of dependent people could become the case managers in the care and community plans. 'The carer often knows the needs of the person being cared for better than any of the professionals' (SSSC, 1990).

This suggestion brings us close to individualised funding and service brokerage. Real choices for people with mental illness and their families can come through control over resources, in the form of credits or cash. Gerry and Vance from Alberta (Chapter 8) control the resources which fund their service. They use an independent service broker to provide information and technical skills like budget management and drawing up contracts (Brandon, 1989). Church and Revell argue for the desirability of the Albertan system but pose the political barriers: 'Why should government give money to people when it's much happier giving money to systems?' (Church and Revell, 1990).

In a small way, Althea (my wife) and myself are already part of the alternative mental illness services. Over more than two decades some people in distress have come to stay in our home for a few days, weeks, months and sometimes years. Only payment for rent and food is involved. Some have formerly been long-stay mental handicap and mental illness patients. We dislike most of the local formal mental illness services and make no contact with them. We are convinced that this unpaid work is part of a huge movement, largely undiscovered and unheralded, offering some distressed people friendship rather than systems and professionalism, relying on ordinary human contact rather than on techniques. It has become increasingly difficult to do work in that unpaid and informal way without the constant interference of a multitude of professionals.

We all drown in a huge, bureaucratic process which continually abuses and marginalises people who are seen as deviant and inadequate economic producers. The mental illness staff stand unconsciously as barriers between people labelled as mentally ill and an ordinary life. In the 'helping professions' we make a living out of the suffering of others. There is nothing dishonourable in that. Dishonour lies in pathologising people who are frequently the victims of major social forces. Frequently, we or the systems which employ us do not and cannot treat those distressed people as if they were our neighbours, our brothers and sisters, our mother and fathers. Until we do, and have structures which both support and encourage, innovation without change will continue.

References

Donald Attwater, *Penguin Dictionary of Saints* (Penguin, 1965).
Peter Beresford and Suzy Croft, *From Paternalism to Participation – Involving People in Social Services* (Open Service Project, 1990).
David Brandon *et al.*, *The Survivors – A Study of Homeless Young Newcomers to London and the Responses Made to Them* (Routledge, 1980).
David Brandon and Noel Towe, *Free to Choose* (Good Impressions, 1989).
Dennie Briggs, chapter 6 in *Dealing with Deviants*, (eds) Stuart Whiteley, Dennie Briggs and Merfyn Turner (Hogarth Press, 1972).
Arthur Brownlea, 'Participation: Myths, Realities and Prognosis', *Social Science and Medicine*, vol. 25, no. 6 (1987) pp. 605–14.

Kathryn Church and David Revell, 'User Involvement in Mental Health Services in Canada', in *Report of Common Concerns – International Conference of User Involvement in Mental Health Services* (MIND, 1990).

David Cohen, *Forgotten Millions – The Treatment of the Mentally Ill – A Global Perspective* (Paladin, 1988).

DSS, *Caring for People: Community Care in the Next Decade and Beyond*, Cm 849 (HMSO, 1989) p. 5.

Brian Davey, personal communication (August 1990).

HMSO, *Caring for People: Community Care in the Next Decade and Beyond*, Cm 849 (November 1989).

M. J. Haveman and M. A. Maaskant, 'Psychiatric Foster Care for Adult Patients: Results of a Study in the Netherlands', *The International Journal of Social Psychiatry* (Spring 1990).

Chris Heginbotham, *The Rights of Mentally Ill People*, The Minority Rights Group Report No. 74 (1987).

Lucy Johnstone, *Users and Abusers of Psychiatry – A Critical Look at Traditional Psychiatric Practices* (Routledge, 1989).

Bill Jordan, *Value for Caring: Recognising Unpaid Carers* (King's Fund, 1990).

Lancashire County Council Social Services Department, *Adult Placement Scheme for People with Learning Difficulties – Policy and Operational Working Document* (1989).

John MacKnight, 'Regenerating Community', Presented before the Canadian Mental Health Associations Search Conference, Ottawa (28 November 1985).

John MacKnight (ed.), *A Story that I Heard*, Pennsylvania Developmental Disabilities Planning Council, 569 Forum Building, Harrisburg, PA 17120 (1986).

MIND/Roehampton Institute, *People First Survey* (1990).

Office of Health Economics, *Mental Health in the 1990s: From Custody to Care* (OHE, 1990).

Shula Ramon, 'Social Work Teams Facing the Closure of a Psychiatric Hospital', unpublished (1990).

Susan B. Rifkin, 'Health Planning and Community Participation', *World Health Forum*, vol. 7, no. 2 (1986) pp. 156–67.

Eugeen Roosens, *Mental Patients in Town Life – Geel – Europe's First Therapeutic Community* (SAGE, 1979).

Salman Rushdie, 'In Good Faith', *The Independent on Sunday* (4 February 1990).

P. O. Sandman, A. Norberg and R. Adolfsson, 'Verbal Communication and Behaviour During Meals in Five Institutionalised Patients with Alzheimer-type Dementia', *Journal of Advanced Nursing*, 13(1988) pp. 571–8.

Secretary of State for Health, Speech to the Royal College of General Practitioners, THS (December 1989).

Peter Sedgwick, *Psycho Politics* (Pluto Press, 1982).

Adam Smith, *The Wealth of Nations* (Edinburgh, 1776).

Helen Smith, 'Collaboration for Change', in David Towell *et al.* (eds), *Managing Psychiatric Services in Transition* (King's Fund, 1989).

Social Services Select Committee, report, *Community Care: Carers* (HMSO, 1990).

Marry van Dongen, *Independent Living*, Helios – Commission of the European Communities Programme for Disabled People (1990).

World Health Organisation, *Consumer Involvement in Mental Health and Rehabilitation Services* (WHO, 1989).

Index